;cotian
community is ~~demolished~~ and fights back

RIGHTING CANADA'S
WRONGS

Africville
An African Nova Scotian Community
Is Demolished — and Fights Back

Gloria Ann Wesley

JAMES LORIMER & COMPANY LTD., PUBLISHERS
TORONTO

Copyright © 2019 by Gloria Ann Wesley and James Lorimer & Company Ltd., Publishers. Published in Canada in 2019.

James Lorimer & Company Ltd., Publishers acknowledges funding support from the Ontario Arts Council (OAC), an agency of the Government of Ontario. We acknowledge the support of the Canada Council for the Arts, which last year invested $153 million to bring the arts to Canadians throughout the country. This project has been made possible in part by the Government of Canada and with the support of Ontario Creates.

Canada   Canada Council   Conseil des arts
           for the Arts   du Canada

ONTARIO ARTS COUNCIL
CONSEIL DES ARTS DE L'ONTARIO
an Ontario government agency
un organisme du gouvernement de l'Ontario

ONTARIO
CREATES

Cover design: Tyler Cleroux

Library and Archives Canada Cataloguing in Publication

Wesley, Gloria, author
        Africville : an African Nova Scotian community is demolished - and fights back / Gloria Ann Wesley.

(Righting Canada's wrongs)
Includes bibliographical references and index.
ISBN 978-1-4594-1358-0 (hardcover)

        1. Africville (Halifax, N.S.)--History--20th century--Juvenile literature. 2. Africville (Halifax, N.S.)--Social conditions--20th century--Juvenile literature. 3. Black Canadians--Nova Scotia--Halifax--Social conditions--20th century--Juvenile literature. 4. Black Canadians--Nova Scotia--Halifax--Relocation--History--20th century--Juvenile literature. 5. Relocation (Housing)--Nova Scotia--Halifax--History--20th century--Juvenile literature. 6. Race discrimination--Nova Scotia--Halifax--History--20th century--Juvenile literature. 7. Halifax (N.S.)--Ethnic relations--History--20th century--Juvenile literature. 8. Halifax (N.S.)--History--20th century--Juvenile literature. I. Title. II. Series: Righting Canada's wrongs

FC2346.9.B6W48 2018   j971.6'22500496
C2018-902579-4

James Lorimer & Company Ltd., Publishers
117 Peter St., Suite 304
Toronto, ON, Canada
M5V 0M3
www.lorimer.ca

Printed and bound in Korea.
Manufactured by We SP. Co., Ltd
Job # 19E-0015

Also in the Righting Canada's Wrongs series

Residential Schools
The Devastating Impact on Canada's Indigenous Peoples

The Chinese Head Tax
and Anti-Chinese Immigration Policies in the Twentieth Century

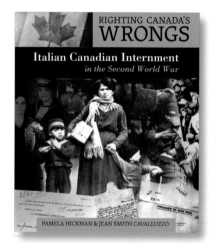

Italian Canadian Internment
in the Second World War

Japanese Canadian Internment
in the Second World War

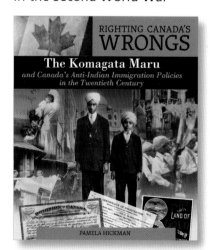

The Komagata Maru
and Canada's Anti-Indian Immigration Policies in the Twentieth Century

To all resilient people who have fought, and who continue to fight, to right the wrongs of racism and bigotry, and who faithfully challenge imbalances of power for justice and quality of life.

Acknowledgements

When the City of Halifax moved forward with its urban renewal program in the mid-1960s, the result was the complete destruction of the city's African Nova Scotian neighbourhood of Africville. The relocation of its 400 citizens meant the end of a vibrant community, resulting not only in feelings of grief, loss and outrage, but also in a legacy of a people's resistance to racism and the workings of the power of the state.

I extend my deepest appreciation to the many individuals, cultural centres, archivists, historians, librarians and journalists for their co-operation and interest in this massive undertaking to ensure the images and stories of Africville are not lost, and supplying their rich resources for me to use in this book.

I would also like to thank James Lorimer, publisher, for his vision and dedication in preserving and keeping stories of injustice alive. I would like to acknowledge Pam Hickman whose guidance and assistance were invaluable during this project as well as Sara D'Agostino, production editor and Tyler Cleroux, design.

Lastly, I wish to acknowledge the invaluable assistance of the following: Irvine Carvery, Eddie Carvery, Paula Smith, Sunday Miller, Lynn Higgins, Wayne Ashe, Kathleen Odusanya, Jennifer Desmond, Shari Shortliffe, Jason Farmer and Sherri Borden Colley. Their contributions, whether utilized or not, were wonderful gestures of their kindness.

A special thanks to my son, Brian Wesley-Daye, for taking many photographs and acting as my chauffeur with enthusiasm and patience.

— G. A. W.

Contents

WATCH THE VIDEO

Look for this symbol throughout the book for links to video and audio clips available online.

Visit www.lorimer.ca/wrongs to see the entire series

Map of Black Settlements in Nova Scotia

This map shows the many communities where Black immigrants / refugees settled in Nova Scotia, including Africville (number 24).

Shelburne
1 Shelburne
2 Birchtown

Yarmouth
3 Yarmouth
4 Greenville

Digby
5 Southville
6 Danvers
7 Hassett
8 Weymouth Falls
9 Jordantown
10 Conway
11 Acaciaville
12 Digby

Annapolis
13 Lequille
14 Granville Ferry
15 Inglewood
    (Bridgetown)
16 Middleton

Kings
17 Southville
18 Gibson Woods
19 Aldershot
20 Kentville

Hants
21 Five Mile Plains

Halifax
22 Beechville
23 Hammonds Plains
24 Africville
25 Lucasville
26 Cobequid Road
27 Halifax
28 Dartmouth
29 Lake Loon
30 Cherry Brook
31 North Preston
32 East Preston

Colchester
33 Truro

Cumberland
34 Springhill
35 Amherst

Pictou
36 Trenton
37 New Glasgow

Antigonish
38 Antigonish
39 Monastery

Guysborough
40 Mulgrave
41 Upper Big Tracadie
42 Lincolnville
43 Sunnyville

Cape Breton
44 North Sydney
45 Sydney
46 New Waterford
47 Glace Bay

Queens
48 Liverpool

Introduction

Diets were easily supplemented by picking fruit, like these blueberries.

The settlement of Africville took place in 1848 when William Brown and William Arnold, Black refugees who fled the War of 1812, became landowners there. Located on the southern shore of the Bedford Basin, Africville was originally known as the Campbell Road Settlement after the road built to connect Bedford Basin to Halifax. Over time Africville grew into a close-knit community. By 1917, Africville had 400 residents, stores, a school, a post office and the Seaview United Baptist Church — its spiritual and social centre.

To former residents it was home, a thriving community where people supported each other, made their own living, had dignity and paid their taxes. Over the years, the city refused to install basic services such as water, sewage and paved roads, and withheld police and fire protection. At the same time, a long list of dangerous and unhealthy industries and institutions were forced on to the site of the Africville community, in what was clearly environmental racism. The people tried to fight back but they lost the battle.

Deacon Ralph Jones ponders the future.

Africville had existed for 120 years when it was demolished by the City of Halifax in the mid-1960s. Its residents were forcibly relocated, many to public housing, as part of the city's urban renewal and desegregation strategies. But Africville residents were not interested in social awareness, reforms or integrating into a city where their culture, values and freedom would be lost. They wanted assistance to improve their existing community so they could remain there.

Activists like Eddie Carvery, a former resident of Africville, began his protest after the last resident, Aaron "Pa" Carvery, left in 1970. Eddie moved a trailer, with "Africville Protest" painted on the side, on to the Africville site. He has been fighting against the wrongs that his family and other residents have suffered as a result of relocation for nearly fifty years.

Even though residents voiced their discontent and demands at meetings on several occasions before, during and after the relocation, their concerns were overlooked and they were given little opportunity to affect the City of Halifax's actions and policy.

Land and homes meant stability and independence.

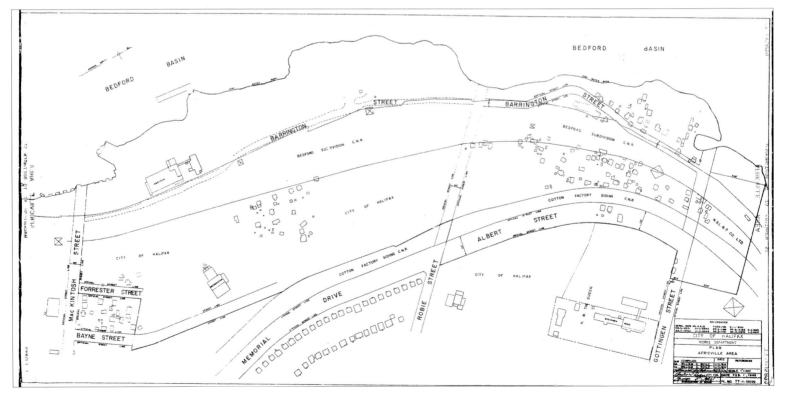

By 1964, the city envisioned Africville gone.

Grassy, open, safe spaces for children to play.

Irvine Carvery was thirteen when the bulldozers came to raze Africville. A strong community activist, he waged an ongoing battle with the Halifax Regional Municipality (HRM). Finally, in 2010, HRM issued an apology for its treatment of Africville residents. Some were satisfied, but many were not. In 2016, a large group of former residents and descendants, including Plaintiffs Nelson Carvery and Tony Smith, joined a lawsuit against HRM over the loss of their land.

The stories told by former Africvillers help us understand what it means to lose a community of free and independent citizens. How, as a result of being a people whose presence, views and skin colour were a recipe for injustice and long-term suffering, they have been left in limbo. Still, nearly five decades later, they remain hopeful for fair compensation for the loss, pain and suffering resulting from their displacement.

Joe Sealy's *Africville Suite* immortalized Africville.

SLAVERY IN THE AMERICAS

In European colonies in North and South America and the Caribbean, landowners found that a cheap labour force was required in order to make growing sugar and cotton profitable. Their solution was to capture humans in West Africa and force them into slavery. Beginning in 1650, Europeans and African slave traders enslaved an estimated eleven to fifteen million Black West Africans and shipped them to North America, South America and the Caribbean where they were sold to landowners.

Captured and Enslaved

Captive West African men, women and children were chained together and forced to walk to the nearest seaport. They were shipped in horrific conditions to the Americas and the Caribbean where they were sold as slaves. A slave has no rights, no protection from abuse and must act as their owner requires under threat of punishment, deprivation or even death.

Valued as a Commodity
Young female slaves, such as the one pictured here, were considered an attractive asset for breeding potential, sexual exploitation and longevity.

Impoverished Living Conditions
Slaves had to rely on their owners for housing or building materials, food and clothing. Their living conditions were crude and often overcrowded.

Field Workers
Entire families worked in plantation fields. The family shown here is harvesting cotton in the southern US in the 1800s. The trans-Atlantic slave trade was made illegal by Britain in 1807, but slavery was not and many countries continued the practice. The *Slavery Abolition Act of 1833* ended slavery throughout the British-controlled world, including Canada, in 1834.

A Nova Scotia Slave Importer
"Just imported and to be sold by Joshua Mauger . . ." reads this ad for slaves in 1762. Mauger was a leading figure in the colony, and was appointed Nova Scotia's Agent in London, England. He traded in liquor and slaves. Many other leading Nova Scotians were slave owners.

Children could be sold and separated from their parents.

Controversial Property
Whole families like this one were captured and enslaved. Children were born into slavery and were required to work once able. Slavery was legal and practised throughout Canada. Some immigrants to Canada brought their slaves with them. Some purchased and imported slaves. However, slavery was opposed by many leading figures. Pictou County's Reverend James MacGregor was a powerful early anti-slavery campaigner from 1788 on. The Nova Scotia legislature repeatedly refused to legalize slavery. By the end of the War of 1812, few slaves were left in Nova Scotia.

Early Black Settlement ▶ WATCH THE VIDEO

Not all Black immigrants to Nova Scotia were slaves, but many were. From 1713 to 1758, 200 Black slaves were living in the French fortress and community of Louisbourg in Cape Breton. More Black slaves were brought to Nova Scotia by New England "Planters" — farmers who took over the land that had been farmed by Acadians before their deportation in 1755. The 1767 Nova Scotia Census listed 104 Black slaves. After 1783, white Loyalists who fled the United States after the revolution brought 1,200 slaves with them to the Maritime colonies. There were also thousands of Black Loyalists, freed by the British during the revolutionary war, who arrived in the 1780s and settled in Halifax, Granville, Clements, Annapolis Royal, Birchtown, Preston, Little Tracadie, Chedabucto and elsewhere. Racism relegated Black people who were free to mainly field and domestic work. According to historian Harvey Whitfield of the University of Vermont, "The Black Loyalists were only nominally free and could easily slip back into a state of slavery. They were Black, like their enslaved brethren, and this racial identity was more significant in deciding their place in society as opposed to whether they were free or not. Free Blacks did not enjoy much freedom . . ." In 1792, 1,196 free Black Loyalists departed Nova Scotia, in fifteen ships, for Sierra Leone, Africa. In 1796, 600 Trelawney Maroons — Black former slaves who had fought an unsuccessful rebellion against the British — arrived in Nova Scotia from Jamaica. Most of them also opted to leave the colony a few years later.

▶ Watch the video at
http://tinyurl.com/rcwafricville01

Loyalist communities
This map shows the locations of settlements of Black Loyalists in Nova Scotia.

Entrepreneurs

Black Loyalist Rose Fortune, shown in this portrait, lived in Annapolis Royal, NS, where she carted luggage, policed property and maintained order on the wharves.

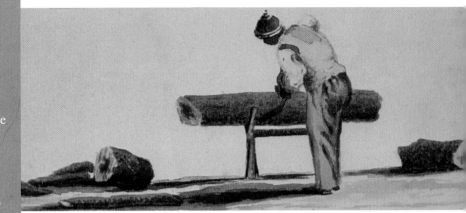

Skilled Worker

This watercolour by Captain William Booth depicts a sawyer in Shelburne in 1788. Both free Black Loyalists and Black slaves brought from America by white Planters and Loyalists lived in Nova Scotia in the 1700s.

Free Black Loyalists and Black slaves lived in Nova Scotia.

Watch the video at
http://tinyurl.com/rcwafricville03

The Maroons — Rebels Against Slavery

Leonard Parkinson, shown in this portrait, was captain of the Maroons — escaped slaves who lived in the hills of Jamaica free of British colonial rule. After a series of uprisings, the Maroons were expelled from Jamaica in 1796 and sent to Nova Scotia. The 600 men, women and children settled in Preston Township. They worked on the roads and for local farmers and merchants. The men helped construct Government House in Halifax, worked on fortifications at the Citadel and served in the militia. The women supplied berries, eggs, poultry, brooms and baskets to the Halifax Market. The Maroons petitioned the government to be returned to Jamaica. Instead, the government transported all of them to Sierra Leone.

WATCH THE VIDEO

Refugees Arrive

WATCH THE VIDEO

During the War of 1812, many African American slaves from Georgia and the Chesapeake Bay coastal regions of Maryland and Virginia saw their chance for freedom by seeking refuge behind British lines. They came to Nova Scotia between 1813 and 1816 on British ships. They settled at Preston, Hammonds Plains, Beechville, Five Mile Plains, Beaver Bank, Prospect Road, Halifax, Dartmouth and elsewhere in the province.

Watch the video at
http://tinyurl.com/rcwafricville02

British Infantryman
This Black soldier was a member of the 104th (New Brunswick) Regiment of Foot, 1810–1817, part of the British Army.

New Arrivals Came by Ship
The "Ship News" column from the *Acadian Recorder* in 1814 announces the arrival of several hundred Black refugees in Halifax.

Refugee Reminder
This gravestone of Private Everett S. Hyson lies in Beechville, NS. He was a descendent of Black Loyalist refugees. They were given five thousand acres (20 km²) of land close to the Northwest Arm in an area later known as Refugee Hill.

On the Move

This painting depicts Black Loyalist refugees on Hammonds Plains Road making their way along the Bedford Basin in 1835. Rather than receiving ownership of land like white settlers, in 1816 the Black refugees were issued "licenses of occupation," meaning they were permitted to stay on the land, but did not own it. In 1834, thirty men at Upper Hammonds Plains received ownership of 600 acres. In 1842, 1,800 acres at Preston was converted from licenses of occupation to ownership. Despite the ongoing hurdles of poverty, racism and poor land, many Black refugees survived, thrived and continued to develop their communities.

"... we beg leave respectfully to suggest that the proportion of Africans already in this country is productive of many inconveniences ..."

Anti-Immigration Politician

In this document from 1815, a member of the Nova Scotia House of Assembly, Peleg Wiswall, opposes Black Loyalist refugee immigration. "We observe with concern, and alarm, the frequent arrival in this Province of Bodies of Negroes, and Mulattoes, of whom many have already become burdensome to the Public." Also, "... we beg leave respectfully to suggest that the proportion of Africans already in this country is productive of many inconveniences, and that introduction of more must tend to the discouragement of white labourers and servants, as well as to the establishment of a separate and marked class of people, unfitted by nature to this climate, or to an association with the rest of his Majesty's Colonials."

107

To His Excellency Lieutenant-General Sir JOHN COAPE SHERBROOKE, Knight Grand Cross of the Most Honourable Military Order of the Bath, Lieutenant-Governor, and Commander in Chief, in and over His Majesty's Province of Nova-Scotia, and its Dependencies, &c. &c. &c.

THE HUMBLE ADDRESS OF THE HOUSE OF REPRESENTATIVES, IN GENERAL ASSEMBLY:

May it please Your Excellency,

WE, His Majesty's dutiful and loyal Subjects, the Representatives of his good people of Nova-Scotia, in General Assembly, beg leave most respectfully, to state to your Excellency, that we observe with concern, and alarm, the frequent arrival in this Province of Bodies of Negroes, and Mulattoes, of whom many have already become burthensome to the Public.

In compliance with your Excellency's humane recommendation, a sum of money is, by this Assembly, placed at your Excellency's disposal, for their temporary relief.

We are well persuaded that these poor people have been cast upon this Province by unforseen events, not in the power of your Excellency to control : But it becomes our duty to state to your Excellency, for the information of such of his Majesty's Officers, as we have not the means of communicating with, that we are unwilling by any aid of ours, to encourage the bringing of Settlers to this Province, whose character, principles and habits, are not previously ascertained.

In the full persuasion, that our most Gracious King, in the exercise of his just prerogatives, will ever consider the interests of his faithful Subjects in this Province ; we beg leave respectfully to suggest, that the proportion of Africans already in this country is productive of many inconveniencies ; and that the introduction of more must tend to the discouragement of white labourers and servants, as well as to the establishment of a separate and marked class of people, unfitted by nature to this climate, or to an association with the rest of his Majesty's Colonists.

Relying upon your Excellency's approved zeal, in behalf of this Province, we humbly pray that your Excellency, will use your endeavours to prohibit the bringing any more of these people, into this Colony, by making such representations to his Majesty's Ministers, as your Excellency may deem proper, or taking such other measures as to your Excellency may seem expedient.

We conclude this Address, with expressing our grateful sense of the attention on all occasions, shewn by your Excellency, for applications made to you, by the Representatives of his Majesty's Subjects in this Province, and with offering our earnest wishes for your Excellency's health and happiness.

Resolved,

Nova Scotia in the 1800s

By 1800, Nova Scotia was a British colony with a small but diverse population. By then, members of the Mi'kmaq First Nation had witnessed the arrival of French, British American and German settlers, as well as Black people of African ancestry, both free and enslaved. For the most part, the diverse communities kept to themselves, separated by race, class, language and culture.

British Influence
Bellevue House, pictured here, was the Halifax residence of the commander-in-chief of the British military from 1801 to 1906. It reflects the British influence that dominated the culture and politics of the British colony of Nova Scotia in the 1800s.

An Inheritance of Slaves

In the early 1800s, even though there was widespread public opposition to slavery, well-off people continued to own slaves. In the 1802 will of Benjamin Belcher of Port Williams, NS, slaves were included in the inventory of his property and bequeathed to his beneficiaries. Two of Belcher's slaves were later among the original settlers of the historic Black communities of Pine Woods and Gibson Woods. Pine Woods was later destroyed when the area was expropriated in 1904 for military use and was renamed Camp Aldershot.

Like Black settlers, the Mi'kmaq faced poverty, racism and oppression.

Mi'kmaq Presence

When Black Loyalist refugees arrived in Nova Scotia, they encountered people of many backgrounds. Pictured here is a Mi'kmaq encampment at Tufts Cove, across the narrow inlet of water from the land that later became the settlement of Africville.

Contrasting Conditions

Like the Black settlers, the indigenous Mi'kmaq faced poverty, racism and oppression in Nova Scotia. Note the contrast in housing conditions documented by this photograph from 1871.

CHAPTER 2
SETTLING AFRICVILLE

The Beginning

Black settlers in Nova Scotia were on the move in the 1800s in search of employment, better land and acceptance. A number of new communities were established around the province. The exact origins of the community of Africville, initially known as Campbell Road, are uncertain, although indications are that the land was previously occupied by white settlers. The earliest record of Black settlers is in 1848, when William Brown and William Arnold obtained legal documents, or deeds, confirming their ownership of fifteen acres of land along the shores of the Bedford Basin — the land that became the site of Africville. Within this area, other pioneering families, including the Carvery, Hill, Fletcher, Dixon, Bailey and Grant families, obtained small lots of land. This Campbell Road settlement of Halifax was quickly dubbed "Africville" due to its largely Black population.

Black Settlement
This 1816 map shows Preston, one of the early Black settlements near Halifax, NS. Some of its residents moved to Africville.

Making Progress
Most of the original settlers of Africville came from other Black settlements in Nova Scotia, including Preston and Hammonds Plains. This photo shows a farmer with a team of oxen in Preston in the late 1800s.

Black worshippers were unwelcome in local churches.

Established Churches
Richard Preston was a slave who purchased his freedom in 1816 and became a plantation preacher in Virginia. He went to Nova Scotia in search of his mother who had arrived as a War of 1812 refugee. Black worshippers were unwelcome in local churches so Preston pushed Black Nova Scotians to build their own churches. He assisted in setting up the Africville church in 1849.

Early Africville

Beginning in the mid-1800s, the building of Africville progressed house by house. New arrivals built shelters on available land. As families expanded, new homes were built close by. In this way, a tight-knit community emerged where neighbours knew each other, supported each other through tough times and shared what they had.

A tight-knit community emerged.

Settling Down
The Africville community grew up along the shore of the Bedford Basin, pictured here in the early 1900s.

Early Homes
Original parcels of land were divided up and filled in with home-made housing, such as the ones pictured here. This 1960s image shows how homes were often added on to over the years and newer homes fitted in close to existing ones as families expanded. No images of Africville homes in the late 1800s or early 1900s exist in the archives.

Lots of Children
A young Africville resident in the early 1900s is shown here. Some children settled in Africville with their parents. Many were born in the community and became life-long residents.

Open-air Baptisms
This image shows a traditional Black Baptist baptism ceremony at Lake Banook, NS, in 1892. Similar ceremonies were also part of the Africville community tradition, where individuals were baptised in the Bedford Basin.

Africville and the Halifax Explosion

▶ WATCH THE VIDEO

At the time of the Halifax Explosion in 1917, Africville had a population of 400. Protected from the explosion by elevated land to the south, Africville suffered considerable damage but houses were not destroyed. Architect Andrew S. Cobb was travelling to Halifax by train on the day of the explosion. A government report said, "When the train stopped near Africville he saw people carrying their injured in sheets . . ." In the aftermath of the disaster, during an enormous civic rebuilding effort, the community received little relief assistance and was excluded from the city's renewal plans.

▶ Watch the video at http://tinyurl.com/rcwafricville05

Damaged Community
These women are walking from Africville towards Halifax on Campbell Road near Hanover Street following the Halifax Explosion. Note the destruction in the background. The Halifax Relief Commission's reports document that Africville suffered damage to homes, the school, church and railway lines.

Receiving Care
An injured woman receives care after the explosion. The Africville community suffered four fatalities and many minor injuries.

Damage and Assistance Denied
A man walks past a wrecked home on Campbell Road. The City of Halifax and the official relief commission considered Africville unaffected though they had documentation of damage. Civic authorities denied it reconstruction aid.

Authorities denied reconstruction aid to the community.

Relief Stations

The image above shows children getting food from a relief station in Halifax, December 1917. Thousands were affected by the devastation of the explosion and needed assistance. Author and historian David Sutherland writes: "When it came to Black families getting help, there is clearly a pattern of racism . . . More subtle forms of discrimination included tagging clients as being 'mulatto' or 'coloured'; hinting at the presence of venereal disease; offering relatively low payment on claims for lost and damaged property; early and arbitrary suspension of food supplies; and the persistent neglect of residents of Africville." Sutherland notes that the Halifax Relief Commission had "no official policy to say that Blacks should be given less relief than whites, but it played favourites."

Kids Carry On

One of the few activities and distractions the children had after the Halifax Explosion was sledding. A major snowstorm followed on the heels of the explosion, increasing the hardship and suffering of the victims. While the adults struggled to cope, these kids managed to find some fun.

Noxious Neighbours

During Africville's lifetime, the City of Halifax permitted or imposed many industrial and noxious facilities in or near the community. These included the Infectious Disease Hospital, Trachoma Hospital, human waste pits, a slaughter house, a city dump, a prison, a bone meal plant, a rolling mill, a nail factory, an incinerator and a stone-crushing plant. In addition, power lines and railway tracks were routed right through the community, dividing it in half. As Africville descendent Denise Allen states, "What they did to Africville is the most blatant and extreme illustration of environmental racism I've ever encountered."

Prison Neighbour
Intermixed with the businesses and noxious industries imposed on the area were city service facilities such as Rockhead Prison, constructed in 1854.

" . . . the most blatant and extreme illustration of environmental racism . . ."

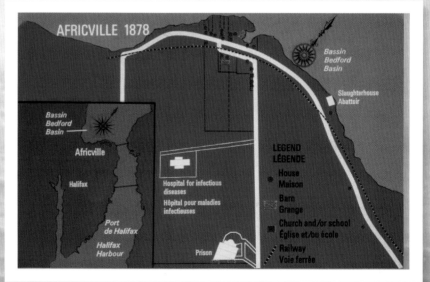

Industrial Growth
This map shows some of the civic and industrial facilities located near Africville in 1878. Others came later.

Early Expropriations
Railway construction through Africville began in 1855. This led to the expropriation of land and relocation of residents without regard for their housing needs or safety, and without payment for the land.

Community Playground
Children are shown here playing on and around the train tracks. They risked being killed by fast-moving trains and some lives were lost.

Taking Over
This image shows the train tracks and hydro towers running through the community. Africville looked like an industrial zone long before the City of Halifax decided on its demolition.

Noxious Neighbours   25

No City Water Service

Pictured here is the water pump at Skinner's Well. In 1852, Halifax City Council agreed to assist in constructing a common well in Africville. Contamination of the wells was so recurrent that residents were continually advised to boil their water before using it for drinking or cooking. Residents protested to the city and petitioned for a municipal water supply, and for sewer service, but they were refused. Residents attributed some serious adverse health effects to the lack of services.

Electrical Towers

Massive electrical transmission towers, shown below, were erected and dispersed throughout the community without consultation or agreement.

"The hospital would just dump their raw garbage on the dump — bloody body parts, blankets, and everything."

Health Hazard

Africville resident Eddie Carvery remembers, "The hospital would just dump their raw garbage on the dump — bloody body parts, blankets, and everything. We were subject to that. And then they would burn this dump every so often. There would be walls of fire and toxic smoke, and we used to run though that fire to get the metals before they melted because we scavenged off the dump. We had to. You had to do that to survive."

Air Pollution

In the mid-1950s, Halifax built an incinerator and a large open civic dump that stretched to within a half mile of Africville. The toxic stench of burning trash was frequent. This image shows the Africville dump on fire.

The Land and the Buildings

WATCH THE VIDEO

In the 1950s and 1960s, Africville was a contained and self-sustaining community where residents eked out their own livings with little help from the outside. What began as a tiny collection of homes grew to support a viable community of hundreds.

Watch the video at
http://tinyurl.com/rcwafricville04

Beauty
Outsiders often termed Africville a slum, but it had many well-cared-for houses and beautiful flower gardens.

Looking Down
This 1965 aerial view of Africville — in the foreground — provides an excellent view of the red-roofed church, the community's houses, the railway tracks and power lines and some of the nearby industrial uses.

Clustered Together
Like many other Nova Scotia neighbourhoods that were built gradually over time from the 1860s to the 1960s, houses were built very close together, filling in available space as the community developed. This Africville hillside offered great views of the Halifax Harbour's Bedford Basin.

It Was Home
Many Africville residents lived on low incomes. Former resident Tony Smith lived in the area called "Africville around the turn." He recalls that the houses were mostly wood-framed and poorly insulated. City services were absent: streets weren't paved and there was no sewer or running water. Residents relied on outhouses and wells.

Irvine Carvery:
"My grandmother was the postmistress
. . . and a lot of the community
things centred at her house because
everyone came there to pick up their
mail."

Postal Services
The white house with the sun porch, pictured here in 1958, was the Africville post office. Irvine Carvery recalls, "My grandmother was the postmistress . . . and a lot of the community things centred at her house because everyone came there to pick up their mail."

Waterfront Views
Flowers and the stunning views of the Bedford Basin are part of the beauty Africville residents recall when describing their former homes.

Comfort and Joy

These pictures of young Irma Sparks, taken inside her home, along with her mother Muriel Sparks preparing a meal, show housing that was typical of Nova Scotia in the 1960s. Former resident Dr. Ruth Johnson recalls, "I was born in a house with plastered walls, a dining room and living room and a butler's pantry and parlour that we were not allowed to go in . . . with the best of furniture. There were lots of lovely homes."

CHAPTER 3

LIFE IN AFRICVILLE

Work Life ▶ WATCH THE VIDEO

Nearly half of Africville's population was under the age of fifteen. The men and women were often limited in their choice of employment due to racism. Men were typically casual labourers employed in seasonal work on coal, grain and salt boats when the St. Lawrence River was frozen. The few tradesmen were mechanics and craftsmen — masons and coopers. Women generally worked as domestics, in a shop or sold handmade goods and produce at the Halifax Market. In 1958, 32 per cent of Africville working men and 60 per cent of women earned less than $1,000 per year, compared to 7 per cent of men and 13 per cent of women in the larger Halifax population.

▶ Watch the video at http://tinyurl.com/rcwafricville06

Christmas Trees
Selling Christmas trees was a traditional seasonal occupation for some men in the Black community. This 1947 image looking up George Street on market day in Halifax shows a man with trees for sale on the back of his horse-drawn wagon.

Working Women
One of the few jobs available to young women was that of a domestic. An 1871 census listed a female workforce of seventy-five in Africville. They were working as cleaners, cooks and washer women.

One of the Few Jobs
Some men found work outside the community. Many became Pullman porters on the trains. Standing here in front of the train for a Royal visit in 1939 are (L-R): John Pannell, Tom MacDonald, Henry Lawrence, J.H. Franklin, George Dixon, R.H. States, B.J. Cromwell and James Spriner.

Dr. Ruth Johnson was born in Africville in 1919: "My father worked on ships. . . Many of the men worked on boats . . . Some of the men worked on the CNR, some worked on the waterfront . . ."

Home Guard Volunteers
In this image, the Home Guard Platoon 7E is posing in front of the Gerrish Street Hall in Halifax in July 1943. This group was made up entirely of African Nova Scotian men and women as part of the Second World War Halifax Civil Emergency Corps. It was a volunteer civilian defence force formed during the war to help provide police, fire, health and various other services in North End Halifax.

Jobs Were Scarce
Tony Smith, shown above, recalls that not everyone had stable jobs.

Tony Smith:
"Some would sell scrap metal to make money. Dump diggers could make $300 to $400 a week. Others relied on seasonal or part-time work to get by."

Dr. Ruth Johnson:
"There were three stores in Africville, what we call penny shops. My mother inherited this store . . ."

Store Owner
Matilda Newman, pictured here in the late 1960s, operated a store out of her home.

Church Life

Seaview African United Baptist Church opened in 1849, and was one of the first five churches set up by Reverend Richard Preston, with Licentiate E. Carvery in charge. The church was the heartbeat of the community. It provided religious services, youth and auxiliary organizations and a connection to other Black churches, often exchanging pastors and preachers. The celebrations gave residents a feeling of solidarity and a collective identity. People gained community status by being involved in church affairs, by acting as official representatives and leaders of the community. Church officials were the authorities who enabled official communiques, petitions and entry into the larger community.

Community Church
Seaview African United Baptist Church, above, was central to all that happened in Africville.

Community Leader
James Robinson Johnston, shown here, was one of the few Black lawyers at the turn of the century. He was prominent in Black organizations and church affairs. His perseverance and drive led to the establishment of a Home and Industrial School for Black children and disadvantaged youth.

Religious Leader
Reverend Donald Skier, shown here, was a well-respected community leader, historian and visiting minister in Africville.

The church was the heartbeat of the community.

Children in the Church
The children pictured are on their way to Sunday School. Elsie Desmond, born in Africville in 1911, recalls, "I went to Seaview Church Sunday School. The deacons were running things, Deacon Edward Dixon and Deacon Arthur Dixon . . . I attended Sunday School at 10 a.m. and services at 11 a.m. and 3 p.m. If we had a special day . . . we had three services."

"We had a great time. We looked forward to it."

Growing Up in the Church
From a young age, Africville children, like those pictured here, received religious instruction and participated in church activities. Stan Carvery, born and raised in Africville, remembers having fun at Christmas concerts at church when he was a boy. "We had a great time. We looked forward to it."

Centre of Community Life

Seaview African United Baptist Church was called "the beating heart of Africville" and was the centre for both church-goers and non-church-goers. The church's baptisms and Easter Sunrise Services were well-known. Both African Nova Scotians and white Nova Scotians would flock to the banks of the Bedford Basin to watch the singing procession leave the church to baptise adults. A former resident recalls the Easter Sunrise Services. "They went into the church singing spirituals around four or five o'clock in the morning when the sun came up and did not come out until 3 p.m."

"It was not just where services were held . . . it was their recreational centre."

Taking Chances

The church grounds were not protected from industrial expansion, with railway tracks running right behind. Terry Dixon lived in Africville until he was thirteen years old. "People in Africville were spiritual. The church was the heart of the community. It was not just where services were held . . . it was their recreational centre."

Church was Everything

Former resident, Brenda Steed-Ross, has vivid memories of the church. "We bury, we marry in it, and any functions people would have there." She said it was also a place where children learned leadership skills from elders, took music lessons and played sports.

Happy Times

In Africville, weddings were often large and beautiful, allowing an opportunity for family to come together from near and far.

Church Life   37

School Life

WATCH THE VIDEO

William Brown, one of the founding members of the community, petitioned the city for financial aid for a school, but was turned down. The *School Act of 1811* excluded the community from access to government funding for education. Until 1883, early Africville residents provided education for their children with the help of a local resident in a one-room schoolhouse. After much more petitioning, the Africville School opened in 1883. The teachers were mostly Black and few had formal training until 1933. Their school closed in 1953 under a provincial move to desegregate the education system. Students then walked to Richmond School. After Grade 8, students were bussed to integrated schools in more affluent neighbourhoods, resulting in many being placed in auxiliary classes from which they never graduated.

Watch the video at
http://tinyurl.com/rcwafricville32

Long-Serving Teacher
Gordon Jemmott Sr., pictured here, taught for twenty-five years in the original school, which started in 1883. His son, Gordon T.C. Jemmott, a graduate of Acadia University, was a teacher, coach and principal of the Africville School for eighteen years.

Africville School
The old schoolhouse, on the shore of the Bedford Basin. It closed in 1953 after seventy years.

It Was a Struggle
Despite parents who stressed the importance of education, school attendance was much lower than enrolment. A 1959 survey by the Institute of Public Affairs revealed that just over 40 per cent of students obtained Grade 6 or less. Only four males and one female reached Grade 10 out of the 140 children registered.

Dedicated Teacher
Portia White, pictured here, studied education at Dalhousie University, graduating in 1929, and became a school teacher in communities such as Africville and Lucasville. She moved on to become the first Black Canadian concert singer to win international acclaim.

```
Elsie Desmond recalls the school:
    "It was a one-room school,
    one door for boys and another
    for girls. I attended until
    I finished Grade 7. It was
    an all-Black school with
    Black teachers. My teacher
    was Mr. Jemmott. He was old
    when he taught us. His son,
    Gordon Jr. and his daughter,
    Melissa, also taught
    school . . ."
```

About 40 per cent of students obtained Grade 6 or less.

In a Hurry
Teens like Brenda Steed-Ross, pictured here on the run, attended high school outside Africville. Classes were integrated with mostly white Halifax students.

Moving to a New School
Hope Carvery is pictured here in 1965. After the Africville school closed, she attended the integrated Richmond School.

Social Life

The church was the centre of many of the community's social interactions. It hosted clubs and recreational activities, especially for youth. Africville men joined many of the after-work Black clubs, organizations and societies in Halifax. Women formed auxiliaries and tea groups. Sports provided the community with social interactions outside Africville, and helped to relieve stress and provided affordable entertainment. Summer sports included stick ball, track and field, horseshoes and baseball — the Rangers men's team and the Africville Ladies' Softball Club. In winter, the Bedford Basin was the site of ice skating, sledding and hockey. The Coloured Hockey League of the Maritimes (1894–1930) produced championship teams like the Africville Brown Bombers and the Africville Sea Sides. Residents were proud of their community and over time developed their unique culture and a huge pool of talent. Reinforcing the community's own sense of achievement and identity, Black entertainer Duke Ellington and boxer Joe Louis visited when they were in Halifax. Meanwhile the wider community characterized Africville as a "slum."

▶ **WATCH THE VIDEO**

Africville Champion
Africville-born George Dixon (1870–1908) was the first Black world boxing champion in any weight, and the first-ever Canadian-born boxing champion. He was posthumously inducted into Canada's Sports Hall of Fame in 1955.

▶ Watch the video at
http://tinyurl.com/rcwafricville33

All-Black Hockey League
The Coloured League All Stars of 1931 are pictured here. The league was formed in Nova Scotia twenty-two years before the National Hockey League. Over 400 African Canadian players played on over a dozen teams.

Many Organizations
The Young Women's Christian Association's (YWCA) Comrade Club, pictured here in the 1930s, sponsored activities in communities throughout the Halifax area.

Growing Families
Rosella Carvery, a former Africville resident, is holding her granddaughter, Deborah Lawrence, in this 1957 photo below.

Ride-em Cowboy
This happy young boy on his pony is all dressed up, perhaps for a special event. Several men owned and used horses for moving and garbage collection in the city.

A Respected Elder
Elders were highly regarded as leaders and mediators in the community. In 1959, only 5 per cent of the population of Africville were sixty and over.

A Fun Time
The Halifax Coloured Citizen's League Annual Picnic, 1965, provided children with activities and good family time.

Good Times
These girls, left, sit and play surrounded by a garden full of gladiolus and the Bedford Basin beyond. In 1959, almost half of the Africville residents were under fifteen.

Learning to Box
B.A. Husbands, far right, was born in Barbados in 1883. He founded the Halifax Coloured Citizens Improvement League, and was president from 1932 to 1968. Recreational facilities for Black youth were a priority and he helped develop the George Dixon Community Recreation Centre. He also fought to get Black people accepted into the nursing profession.

Berry Picking
A group of children pick wild blueberries in Africville in this 1960s photo. Blueberries provided extra income and were plentiful and free.

Tony Smith recalls growing up in Africville:
"I used to fish from the rocks and play on an old tugboat. Kids would boil periwinkles and mussels to eat; they went eel fishing at night and made bonfires; they picked blueberries, apples and built forts in the woods."

Happy Times
Children at play
in Africville.

Early Paddleboard?
Africville children swam, rafted and fished in the nearby Bedford Basin. With plenty of materials available from the dump, this group made their own rafts.

"**Living in Africville at that time was more like a dream . . . It was like a resort in the back of the yard.**"

— Leo Carvery, born in Africville in 1916

Social Life

CHAPTER 4

DEMOLITION

Neglected and Threatened

From the time Africville was settled, the community did not receive treatment equal to that provided to other taxpayers in Halifax. It took many protests and petitions before residents obtained their own school, post office, street lights and street numbers. Other issues like the nearby dump, noxious industries close by, lack of public services such as water, sewers, paved roads and police protection, were never addressed. Halifax residents noticed the condition of the community and blamed the residents, terming the area a "slum," denying that it was the municipal government that played the largest role in creating substandard conditions. Without basic services, Africville's residents were mistrustful of the city and angry at what is now recognized as environmental racism.

In 1917, the city had considered, then shelved, plans to turn Africville into an industrial zone. In 1945, the Civic Planning Commission recommended the removal of the Africville community. Halifax City Council revived the shelved 1917 plans in 1947 and approved rezoning Africville as industrial land.

The Decision Makers
As early as 1855, several Africville families were forced to move to make way for development. An 1860 petition from William Brown to the city included a request for compensation for land taken. When railway trustees provided replacement land to some relocatees, they did not give these former property owners ownership of the land until five years later. In 1901, five families were forced to move to make way for additional railway tracks. By 1907 the Halifax City Council, pictured here in 1903, had acquired land on all sides of Africville.

Africville Not Policed

The photo above shows the Halifax City Police on the Grand Parade in 1914. Policing was not extended to Africville, even after several petitions for service had been made. Nevertheless, the 1945 Halifax Master Plan said of "slums": "The cost of providing fire, police, medical, social and other services in such areas is always higher than for other sections. On the other hand, the tax revenue from these areas is disproportionately low. The entire community thus subsidizes the maintenance of slums." No acknowledgement was made of the failure to provide these services to these communities.

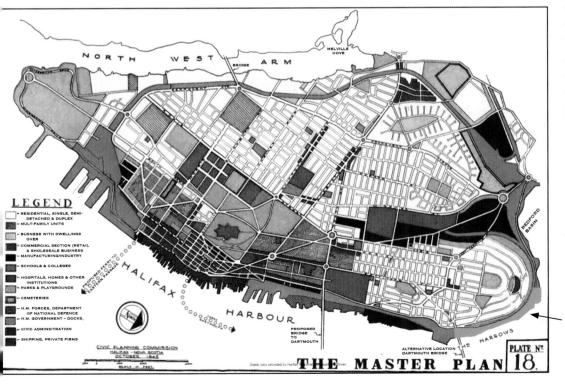

Africville

The Master Plan

The City of Halifax's 1945 Master Plan, pictured here, was the first effort at city planning. The plan was overwhelmingly concerned with decreasing widespread social problems throughout the city's North End through zoning. The plan contained fifty-two recommendations, including guidance for addressing slum conditions. The removal of the "Africville settlement" located on the southern shore of the Bedford Basin, was part of an overall plan to widen Barrington Street along the railway line, with the provision of "a decent minimum standard of housing elsewhere" for the residents.

Advocating for the Community

As early as the mid-1800s, residents of Africville petitioned the City of Halifax for basic services that were available just up the road. Over the years, they requested compensation for land that was expropriated for railways and other facilities. They fought for a school, policing and fire protection and many other improvements that the city had denied them. The residents were not passive victims. The community leaders continued to push for better living conditions until the end.

To His Worship The Mayor and members of the City Council
Gentlemen We the undersigned residents of the community of Africville beg to present our petition for a Public ... for the use of our Village
A recent automobile accident and other causes destroyed our only available water supply for cooking drinking and ablutionary purposes. Physical ... and Sanitary considerations therefore combine to emphasize the need of a sufficient water supply for the above purposes
We therefore beg you honorable council to take such prompt and effective ... as will grant unto us the prayer of this memorial and your petitioners as in duty bound ... ever pray ...
Executed this 19th day of July a.d. 1909

1909 Petition
This petition illustrates the civic activism of Africville residents.

Africville's Leading Advocate
B.A. Husbands, shown here, made representation to the city authorities on issues like education, housing and recreation. He was a strong advocate for Africville and for the betterment of all Black Nova Scotians. The city opened a school in Africville in 1883. It was closed in 1953 along with many other Black schools because the province was desegregating its education system.

A Place to Go
The Home for Coloured Children, pictured here, provided industrial, business, and domestic training for Black people, and shelter for orphans and destitute Black children. After the original house in Halifax was destroyed in the 1917 explosion, a new home was opened in 1921 in Westphal, Dartmouth.

Boil this Water
Africville residents petitioned the city for a public well in 1909. Their only available water supply for cooking, drinking and washing purposes had to be boiled before using. A contaminated water supply continued to plague the community into the 1960s.

Urban Renewal — A National / Provincial / Local Policy

Urban renewal and building public housing was common public policy in the 1940s–1960s in American and Canadian cities. In 1954, a report by the Halifax City manager to the City Council included a mix of these popular ideas, including social integration, urban renewal (which meant demolishing old neighbourhoods and redeveloping them, often with public housing) and "slum clearance." Across Canada, neighbourhoods facing urban renewal were fighting to save their communities and improve civic services. In Halifax, proposals to save the Africville community and improve the community's economic and social conditions were not given credibility. The federal government offered cities funds to help pay the costs of urban renewal. In 1956, the city engaged Dr. Gordon Stephenson to identify areas for urban renewal. In 1957, the City Council adopted a motion to begin expropriation for one mile along the Bedford Basin, including Africville. In a 1962 interview, Mayor John Edward Lloyd said, "Sometimes, some people need to be shown that certain things are not in their own best interests or in the interest of their children . . ."

Father of Change
In 1956, the City of Halifax commissioned University of Toronto professor Gordon Stephenson, pictured here, to conduct an urban renewal study of downtown Halifax. His job was to investigate housing conditions and needs, and to recommend redevelopment policies for Halifax.

A REDEVELOPMENT STUDY OF HALIFAX NOVA SCOTIA · 1957

Stephenson Report
Stephenson was considered an expert in urban renewal and applying scientific precision to justify his findings. The 1957 Stephenson Report, shown here, produced recommendations for urban renewal for Halifax, including removal of the Africville "slum." His report states, "In what may be viewed as an encampment, or shack town, there live some seventy Negro families . . . There are only two things to be said. The families will have to be relocated in the near future. The land which they now occupy will be required for the future development of the city."

Where to Start
This 1962 aerial photo shows the demolished Central Redevelopment Area in Halifax. The Scotia Square shopping centre and office complex was one of Halifax's urban renewal projects.

Relocation Supporter
Allan O'Brien, Halifax City Alderman in 1962, reflected on the relocation process, "... that was a time when the currents in the wind of public opinion had to do with the questions of housing conditions, integration or desegregation, and we felt on the council that a lot needed to be done in Halifax."

New Department Formed
In 1961, the City of Halifax's Housing Policy and Review Committee created the Development Department with responsibility for the demolition of Africville. Development Officer R.B. Grant perceived the area as an environmental disaster. In this image below, housing officials inspect a property.

"The families will have to be relocated in the near future."

Community Response

The premise that Africville residents were "disadvantaged citizens" instead of a specific "interest group" influenced how they were treated. Initially not consulted, and excluded from the planning process, they were in a precarious situation without financial or legal resources and no political clout. But the people of Africville wanted to stay put and called for the development of their community. In 1961, they appealed to Sid Blum, a celebrated community campaigner with the Canadian Labour Congress. He advised the residents to form a ratepayers' association, a group of residents in Africville who would address issues affecting their community. He also asked Alan Borovoy, a lawyer with the National Committee on Human Rights, to visit Halifax and help organize a defence. Borovoy concluded his visit in August 1962, believing relocation was inevitable and stressing the importance of racial integration. He opposed the restoration of Africville as a community. His efforts turned to making the best possible deal for the residents.

Watch the video at
http://tinyurl.com/rcwafricville34

Africville Advocate Joe Skinner
"I think we should have a chance to redevelop our own property as well as anybody else. When you are in this country and you own a piece of property, you're not a second-class citizen. That's why my people own this land . . . they toiled for it. It is land that they own, and they try to hang on to it. But when your land is being taken away from you, and you ain't offered nothing, then you become a peasant — in any man's country."

Favoured Change
Gus Wedderburn, shown here, was an advocate for resettlement. He co-chaired Halifax's Human Rights Advisory Committee (HHRAC) during the 1960s. The committee was to monitor and protect the interests and rights of the people of Africville during the relocation. They sought to amend the terms and conditions of the removal and urge the provincial government to improve the enforcement of human rights law.

Community Leader
Deacon Ralph Jones, pictured above, spoke at the Seaview Church meeting in 1962 in response to the city's July 1962 Development Report recommending the destruction of Africville. During the meeting, Africville residents stated their opposition to relocation. Deacon Jones decried from his pulpit, "If ever there was ever a time to stand by your guard, the time is now! This is testin' time!"

Talking it Over
HHRAC, pictured here in a meeting with Alan Borovoy at the Halifax Hotel in 1962, had ten members, both Black and white. Only three of them — Mr. and Mrs. Peter Edwards and Frank MacPherson, were from Africville. Reverend W.P. Oliver, Buddy Daye, Gus Wedderburn and three city aldermen (Ian MacKeigan, Lloyd Shaw and Don MacLean) were a white-Black alliance known as "caretakers." They saw themselves as protectors of the residents' interests. They were against racial segregation and believed in integration. Over a six-year period, the committee met forty times.

Deal Maker
A community activist in Halifax's North End, Canadian super featherweight title holder Buddy Daye, seen here, was a staunch supporter of Africville and an avid opponent of relocation.

Residents Were Misled
According to lawyer Robert Pineo, pictured here, the city gave residents the impression they had no legal leg to stand on, when in fact the opposite was true. According to the city charter, officials should have told the residents their rights, provided them with legal advice, and offered them fair market value for their properties. "This was not explained to them at the time. Their understanding of the matter was the city had the power to acquire their lands unilaterally and there was no recourse available to them, and no means or process by which to contest the amount of the compensation, if any, that they were assigned."

Community Participation
Younger participants are pictured here at a public meeting at Seaview Church. From 1962 to 1967, HHRAC held seven meetings with residents. A total of seventy-one residents attended the meetings, however attendance at each meeting was low.

Community Response

Buyout and Demolition of Africville

▶ WATCH THE VIDEO

HHRAC suggested that the city engage Dr. Albert Rose, the University of Toronto social work professor and urban renewal expert, to report on Africville and make his recommendation. Rose advocated demolition and relocation, recommending that the services of a lawyer and a social worker be provided to the residents of Africville free of charge, that compensation be negotiated with each family and that a post-relocation package, including job training and employment assistance, be offered over several years. The Rose Report was discussed at a meeting in Seaview Church in January 1964 and was approved in principle by thirty-seven of the forty-one people in attendance. The low turnout of residents meant that the majority of the community was not fully aware of what was offered or agreed upon. The city endorsed the report and agreed on two types of compensation: payment for expropriated land and buildings and relocation assistance. Most community members felt they had no way to challenge the decision.

▶ Watch the video at
http://tinyurl.com/rcwafricville09

What's it Worth?
Peter MacDonald, a social worker appointed by the city, visited each home in Africville and negotiated a financial deal. HHRAC remained involved as a watchdog to ensure fairness and to advise residents. However, only those who had legal documents that proved they owned their property were eligible to negotiate a land settlement. The remaining residents were supposed to be granted a blanket sum of $500 each to relinquish their "squatters' right" to their land. Families also received payment for the city's estimate of the value of the buildings they had lived in.

New Housing
Officials, such as those pictured here, inspected homes before demolition. At the same time, the city was working on the Uniacke Square housing project for relocated Africville residents.

In addition to negotiating financial compensation, city social worker Peter MacDonald also arranged for housing in Halifax, help with moving, welfare assistance and education and employment programs. A Black member of HHRAC spoke about the process. "I don't think they [city officials] give a damn about Black people in Halifax. [We] have never been a group to reckon with. We have never been a political power. We never had a pressure group. We never had money. We were just damn nuisances."

Land Title

The city agreed to compensate property holders at "full market value," however doing so was controversial and difficult. Ownership of the land was often not formally documented. Informal ownership arrangements were common and were respected by the community. Eighty per cent of the land in Africville was already owned by the city, expropriated by the Canadian National Railway and Halifax's "Industrial Mile" in 1957 without informing residents.

City neglect also meant its tax rolls were no help in clarifying property ownership. Africville properties were not assessed regularly, or at all, until after 1956. Even then, because of the uncertainty around title, the city only evaluated the value of the buildings, not the land they sat on. In all, only fourteen of the community's nearly 400 residents had registered deeds for their properties. Eleven of the fourteen had not been clearly plotted and, in two cases, the boundaries were so vague that it was not possible to locate the property.

Arriving at an amount was not a matter of applying a formula. Instead, the city's negotiator calculated what he considered "a fair and equitable settlement" taking into account whether the individuals involved were elderly, had dependent children, what their source of income was and what debts they had — particularly for back taxes or hospital care. The debts were subtracted from the settlement amount. Then an amount for appliances or furnishings in their new lodgings was added as a "furniture allowance." The total was the compensation package provided by the city.

Negotiations went family by family or one by one. The city was required to publish settlement amounts in the newspaper. It did so by property number, rather than the names of the owners, in an attempt to avoid neighbours comparing compensation offers.

A Sad Sight
Houses slated for demolition, such as Deacon Ralph Jones's home, pictured here in 1965, were boarded up first.

"In any negotiation the unique situation of Africville must be given special weight by the civic administration and the people of Halifax."

— The Rose Report, 1963

WATCH THE VIDEO

Forced Moves

City movers are seen here moving Dorothy Carvery. Residents complained about being moved in big yellow city garbage trucks.

```
One relocatee exclaimed:
    "City people sent
    trucks to remove
    my furniture. Just
    think what the
    [new] neighbours
    thought when they
    looked out and saw a
    garbage truck drive
    up and unload the
    furniture."
```

Beginning of the End

The city used garbage trucks like this one to move people and household goods. One resident said of the experience, "I can remember trucks coming in. I remember Mrs. Sarah Mantley's house — they tore it down, they never gave her time to take a stitch of furniture out of her house and they knocked it down. They bulldozed it."

Watch the video at
http://tinyurl.com/rcwafricville10

"Can a minority group be permitted to reconstitute itself as a segregated community . . . at a time in the social history of western industrialized urban nations, when segregation either de jure [in law] or de facto [in fact] is almost everywhere condemned?"

— The Rose Report, 1963

Taking Care

Dorothy Carvery is pictured here carrying some of her belongings. Not everyone was present on moving day.

One resident recalls:
"Mr. James Stewart was in Camp Hill Hospital and they bulldozed the house down. The man didn't even know. He came out of the hospital and had no place to go."

Loading it Up

The city's strategy was to remove those residents who were willing to relocate as quickly as possible and to demolish their buildings immediately, in order to underscore the point that the demolition of Africville was well underway. As each family moved out, their home was instantly demolished. Ultimately, those who refused to move had their land seized.

Tony Smith, a former resident, talks about the loss of Africville: "What I know is the city basically — and this comes with race — they seen this community up in the North End and they thought it was an eyesore and they didn't want it to be there anymore and they just wanted to get rid of it. They knew they could abuse their authority, it didn't matter what anybody says — they were just going to take it."

Fast and Furious

Residents had little time to prepare due to the swiftness and inattention to detail when they were subjected to forced evacuations.

Destroying a Community

From 1964 onward, one by one, the houses in Africville were demolished, and by 1970 Africville was gone. The photo on the right from 1965 shows a demolished house among those still standing. Former resident Irene Izzard-Mantley comments, "Without mercy the government bulldozed our homes in our absence without our permission, and without compassion. They left our grandmothers without shelter at a time when they were most vulnerable and alone — my grandmother was eighty-seven years old when the city bulldozed her home and destroyed all of her belongings. She was left with just one change of clothes amidst the rubble and ruin. Before she died, she made me vow to make the guilty pay. This is the horror I carry to this day."

WATCH THE VIDEO

Demolishing the Church

Africville resident Laura Howe recalled, "I remember my son coming home one night and he said, 'Mom, the church is gone,' and I said, 'Oh no, no, it can't be . . .' It was done in the early hours in the morning. It seemed to me to be a cruel thing to do to a church." The church had been demolished November 20, 1967. This was a devastating and calculated blow to the spirit of the community. "It hurt a lot of the older people," recalls Stan Carvery, another former resident.

Watch the video at
http://tinyurl.com/rcwafricville11

"This is the first time in a quarter-century of slum clearance, public housing and redevelopment activity in North America, that the removal of a severely blighted area will take away from a large proportion of the residents, not merely their housing and their sense of community, but their employment and means of livelihood as well."

— The Rose Report, 1963

Aaron Carvery:

"They sent for me and when I got there I was taken into someone's office. There were five or six persons in the room plus a suitcase full of money all tied up neatly in bundles. The suitcase was open and stuck under my nose so as to tempt me and try and pay me off right there and then. I didn't like that at all. It hurt me. I told them, 'You guys think you're smart, well, you're not smart enough.' Then I got up and walked out of the office. When they finally paid me it was by cheque and they came to my home to do business."

Africville Vanished
This 1969 aerial view of the Bedford Basin shows, in the bottom centre, the razed community of Africville along the railway tracks. A Black community that had existed for 125 years had disappeared from the Halifax landscape.

"There is a very real danger that the dislocation attendant upon expropriation and relocation will be so disruptive of existing living patterns that many more families will require and seek public assistance."

— The Rose Report, 1963

What Happened to the Land?

The land, so cherished by Africville residents, was reused in several ways by the City of Halifax. Some land was used for footings for a new bridge across the harbour. Some was used for industries, such as the Fairview Cove Container Terminal. Some became an off-leash public dog park called Seaview Park.

Repurposing Africville
Footings for the A. Murray MacKay Bridge over Halifax Harbour were built on former Africville land. The bridge, pictured here, was officially opened in 1970.

Land Reuse
The Fairview Cove Container Terminal, which opened in 1982, is part of the industrial expansion along the shores of Halifax Harbour adjacent to former Africville land.

"To think that [the city government] hated us so much that they destroyed our community so dogs could run free."

Dogs Instead of People
Seaview Park, pictured here, was originally designated an off-leash dog park. After petitioning by the Africville Heritage Trust, the City Council changed the designation in 2014 to require owners to leash their dogs. Dr. Ruth Johnson was in her fifties when her home was levelled. "To think I lost my birthplace to a park. To think that they [the city government] hated us so much that they destroyed our community so dogs could run free."

Where Did People Go?

Africville disappeared and its people scattered — some into crowded, newly constructed public housing, some into derelict housing, some purchased homes in Halifax and others moved to different areas of the county and across Canada. While Halifax City saw the relocation as a positive action for a destitute community, others saw it as another occasion for whites to take what they wanted while discounting the lives of Africville residents. The people of Africville lost their homes, businesses and livelihoods, but the biggest loss was their sense of community, their circle of support and the comfort of belonging.

Crowded Spaces
Uniacke Square, above, opened in 1966 as a 250-unit public housing project, built to house the displaced population of Africville.

Social Housing
The high rise pictured here is part of the new Uniacke Square expansion. Sunday Miller, former director of the Africville Museum, said, "When they took them off this land and forced them to be a ward of the government, which is what happened for those who went into social housing, you took their dignity from them."

Evolving Community
Gottingen Street, Halifax, pictured here in 2017, is home for some former Africville residents and their descendants, but Uniacke Square has evolved into a multicultural area.

"... for those who went into social housing, you took their dignity from them."

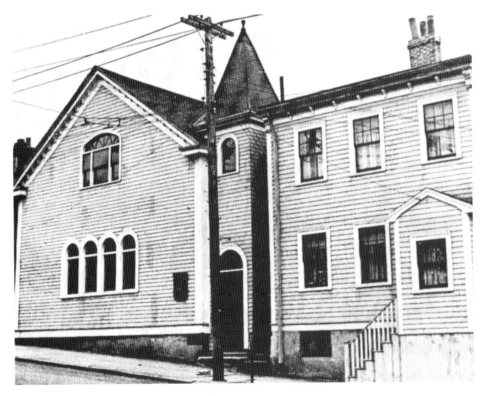

Finding a New Church Community
Having lost Seaview African United Baptist Church, Africville residents who relocated to North End Halifax joined the Cornwallis Street Baptist Church, shown here, which was established in 1832. It was renamed the New Horizons Baptist Church in 2018.

Getting Organized

The education and employment programs and the "home for a home" deals that Africville residents were promised never materialized. The money received for their property was barely enough for a down payment on a new home or to cover a few months' rent. Jobs were difficult to come by, as many companies refused to hire Black people. Former residents lobbied for more compensation and welfare benefits. The city's response was to provide short-term help and to encourage them to form a committee. In 1968, the Seaview Credit Union was formed with a provincial contribution of $50,000 and the city's input of $20,000. The funds were mismanaged and a new group — the Africville Action Committee — formed in 1969. It eventually faded away from lack of resources and experienced leaders, and from the exhaustion of constantly having to combat indifference, legal objections and bureaucratic red tape.

Coming Together
What the former residents lacked in adequate restitution, they more than made up for in spirit. The first church service, spiritual revival and reunion picnic since relocation were held in Seaview Park in 1972. Shown here at that event, from left to right are: Ardith Pye, Mae West, Laura Howe, Elsie Desmond and Althea Mantley.

Determined
A tireless worker, Linda Mantley helped organize the first reunion gathering in 1972. "We're celebrating it because the church was the focal point. That's where all the meetings were taking place when the people were fighting to keep their homes and so we're celebrating the legacy from all the people out home."

Passing on Traditions

Children at the Africville Reunion, 1983. Thousands of people from across Canada and the US joined in the festivities. Elders told stories about their experiences. There were activities for children, a gala dinner, dance and an annual church service.

Never Giving Up
Eddie Carvery, pictured here, continues his decades-long fight for proper compensation. He moved into a "protest trailer" (below) on the Africville site after the last house was demolished in 1970. He has become known as "The Hermit of Africville."

Keeping Africville Relevant

A number of Black organizations supported the Africville community in its struggle for compensation. Dr. Henry Bishop, shown here, was employed as curator at the Black Cultural Centre for Nova Scotia in 1983. He helped organize the 1989 Mount Saint Vincent University (MSVU) Africville Conference. He also co-curated the nationally travelled exhibit, "Africville: A Spirit that Lives On" in 1985.

Reverting Back to Africville

In 2011, a new sign was unveiled as part of the annual Africville Family Reunion. Seaview Park in North End Halifax was officially renamed Africville.

Africville Genealogy Society

Africville may have disappeared as a community, but former residents worked hard to keep the memory and culture alive and perpetuate "the spirit of Africville" for themselves and their descendants. In 1983, the Africville Genealogy Society formed. Its aim is to track former residents and their descendants, bring them together through annual picnics, hold five-year reunions and recognition benefits and be involved with youth. The society advocated for compensation and a memorial to Africville, taking on the City of Halifax (later Halifax Regional Municipality), the Province of Nova Scotia and the Government of Canada.

Deborah Dixon-Jones:
"I wanted to create something that would keep the sense of community that was at the heart of the spirit of Africville alive for the generations still to come."

Celebrating Family
The Africville Reunion, 1983, is pictured here. Reunions keep the memory of Africville alive and ensure children and adults maintain family ties and continue to celebrate their culture. Many families return to the site of their former homes.

Dedicated to Preserving
Africville Genealogy Society founding members were (L-R) Deborah Dixon-Jones, Linda Mantley, Brenda Steed-Ross and Irvine Carvery.

NOTABLE NOVA SCOTIANS
Community Activist
Deborah Dixon-Jones
1949-1989
Africville
One of the three founding members of the Africville Genealogy Society. She is remembered fondly by the other two co-founders of the Society, Linda Mantley and Brenda Steed Ross, as a driving force in the creation of the Africville Genealogy Society.

NOTABLE NOVA SCOTIANS
Community Activist
Linda Mantley
Africville
One of the three founding members of the Africville Genealogy Society and current Secretary/Treasurer of the Society. Active community volunteer lovingly known as Nan by many children in her community.

NOTABLE NOVA SCOTIANS
Community Activist
Brenda Steed Ross
Africville
One of the three founding members of the Africville Genealogy Society. The work of the Society led to the creation of the Africville Heritage Trust.

NOTABLE NOVA SCOTIANS
Community Activist
Irvine Carvery
Africville
President of the Africville Genealogy Society and a Director of the Africville Heritage Trust. Active community volunteer. Recipient of numerous honours and awards including the Queen's Golden Jubilee Medal.

WATCH THE VIDEO

Everyone Welcome

Africville Reunion, 1984. Laura Howe, Stanley Carvery, Beatrice West-Wilkins, Brenda Steed-Ross, Hope Johnston, Linda Carvery, Nelson Carvery and Elsie Desmond hold the banner. Irvine Carvery reflected, "When we return to those grounds, we see it as it was … When I'm talking with my grandchildren, they can visualize better now. There's something tangible to really bring the point home for them."

Watch the video at
http://tinyurl.com/rcwafricville35

WATCH THE VIDEO

Former residents worked hard to keep the memory and culture alive.

Progress Vs. Preserving

Africville reunions bring people back together. Brenda Steed-Ross, pictured here, remembers, "Some of us had already started going out there on our own from time to time, just to have picnics or go fishing or whatever so we could spend some time out home again."

Watch the video at
http://tinyurl.com/rcwafricville14

Not All Peaceful
Sergeant Craig Smith, RCMP, author and community spokesperson, has written about the racist attitudes faced by Black people in North End Halifax when the 1991 Halifax Riot broke out.

WATCH THE VIDEO

Watch the video at
http://tinyurl.com/rcwafricville12

Sergeant Craig Smith:
"The whole idea of Black men being denied access or there being different rules put in place for them when they were going to clubs was a long-held thing."

A leading advocate for the Nova Scotian Black community, Dr. William Pearly Oliver believed that by pursuing education, acquiring skills, celebrating Black culture and learning about Black contributions to society, discrimination would be eradicated and Black people would more easily integrate into Canadian society. His efforts led to opening the Black Cultural Centre in Cherry Brook in 1983.

Never Forget
Continued inaction by the city brought five people together: Mary Spalding, director of the MSVU Art Gallery; Shelagh Mackenzie, a National Film Board producer; Bridglal Pachai, director of the NS Black Cultural Centre; Henry Bishop, curator and Don Clairmont, a Dalhousie University sociologist. They organized a major exhibit and conference at MSVU in 1989. Their goal was to broaden the public perception of Africville from a slum to a living community full of love with an everlasting spirit deserving of compensation for the wrongs done to it. Dr. Ruth Johnson is pictured here speaking at the conference.

AFRICVILLE

A SPIRIT THAT LIVES ON — UNE ÂME TOUJOURS VIVANTE

An exhibition organized by the Art Gallery, Mount Saint Vincent University in collaboration with the Africville Genealogy Society, the Black Cultural Centre for Nova Scotia, and the National Film Board, Atlantic Centre

Une exposition organisée par la Galerie d'art de la Mount Saint Vincent University en collaboration avec la Société généalogique d'Africville, le Centre culturel Noir de la Nouvelle-Écosse et l'Office national du film, région de l'Atlantique

THE AFRICVILLE EXPERIENCE LESSONS FOR THE FUTURE
A CONFERENCE, HIGHLIGHTED BY THREE MAJOR PANELS, FREE AND OPEN TO THE PUBLIC, IN CONJUNCTION WITH THE EXHIBITION
Africville — A Spirit That Lives On

Auditorium C, Seton Academic Centre Mount Saint Vincent University Halifax, Nova Scotia
17 and 18 November, 1989
8 pm Friday, 17 November

The Decision Makers: Why They Did What They Did,
chaired by Carolyn Thomas, African United Baptist Association, brings together some of the key players in the decisions taken between 1964 and 1970
10 am Saturday, 18 November

The Africville Response: How It Felt Then and How It Feels Now,
presents a range of voices from within the community, chaired by Brenda Steed-Ross, a founding member of the Africville Genealogy Society
1:20 pm Saturday, 18 November

A presentation by the Honourable Ronald Giffin, Minister of Education for Nova Scotia
1:30 pm Saturday, 18 November

Lessons From the Experience,
recommendations for change by people affected in various ways, chaired by the Reverend Charles Coleman, a former Africville pastor

Organized by the Africville Genealogy Society, the Black Cultural Centre for Nova Scotia, the Art Gallery, Mount Saint Vincent University, and the National Film Board, Atlantic Centre

Staying Focused
Dr. Ruth Johnson's 1940s black-and-white linocut prints of Africville were featured on the MSVU Conference poster in 1989. Speaking at the conference she said, "The city was very dirty and they got the uneducated ones to say, 'Oh a couple hundred dollars is good for you. You can take that and live in the city.' They [Africvillers] were down there living and minding their own business because they didn't need anybody else. My father fished in the Basin and got all our codfish and salted it down. We had dories and everything. Life was good."

Celebrating in Song
The a capella quartet, Four the Moment, whose songs were fearlessly political, performed at the Africville Conference and Exhibition in 1989.

Lots to Discuss
The Africville Conference and Exhibition Agenda, 1989. The conference allowed community members to express how they felt during relocation twenty years later. The decision-makers also got to explain the process of negotiating the "deal" and why things happened the way they did. Nova Scotia Education Minister Ron Giffin admitted, "... I am as aware as anyone of the racism that exists in our society."

"I am as aware as anybody of the racism that exists in our society."

Africville Genealogy Society

CHAPTER 6

ACKNOWLEDGING THE PAST

First Steps

In late 1991, former residents were jubilant when the province promised to spend $200,000 to build a replica of Seaview Church and to preserve the site of Africville. However, discussions between representatives of the Africville Genealogy Society (AGS) and the City of Halifax stalled. In March 1996, an Action and Statement of Claim was filed against the city. The estates of forty-eight deceased individuals, along with seventy-nine living individuals, were listed as plaintiffs. The claim alleged that Halifax owed the plaintiffs for a broad array of unlawful conduct and breaches of contract over the span of the community's existence. The action sought court orders to set aside the transfer of the land to Halifax, together with damages for the loss and injury suffered because of Halifax's actions. For five years after filing the claim, little progress was made. Negotiations were restarted in 2001 in hopes of finding a resolution outside the courts. To settle the litigation required for a suitable memorial for Africville, a committee was formed in 2005 with representatives from the community and all three levels of government.

Recognition Only

For many, the official plaque, pictured here, represented progress, but not everyone was excited: ". . . if you think I should welcome and be grateful for Africville being designated an historical site, you're wrong," commented former resident Ruth Johnson.

Watch the video at http://tinyurl.com/rcwafricville17

Actions Declared Racist

A 2004 United Nations Report by Mr. Doudou Diene on race relations in Canada, pictured here, stated that the treatment and destruction of Africville was a crime against humanity and urged Canada to consider paying reparations. This put pressure on HRM to move forward with a settlement.

"... we do not owe anybody anything."

Unapologetic Mayor
Walter Fitzgerald, mayor of Halifax from 1971 to 1974, pictured here, maintained that the community had been properly compensated. "The city, according to the records, paid everybody for the land they took in the Africville area and it was all done without expropriation so we do not owe anybody anything. The deal was made, signed, sealed and delivered. People took their money and left. Game over as far as I'm concerned."

"... the treatment and destruction of Africville was a crime against humanity."

— 2004 United Nations report

WATCH THE VIDEO

Hardened Advocate
As president of the AGS, Irvine Carvery, shown here, played an instrumental role in securing official redress. "The real shame of the whole Africville question is what it did to the people — what it took away from the people. We have to put in place some concrete steps to fix some of the ills that have been the result of that discrimination and racism we have had to endure."

 Watch the video at
http://tinyurl.com/rcwafricville15

The Halifax Apology

In December 2006, consultants were engaged to prepare a feasibility study and business plan for the reconstruction of Seaview United Baptist Church and the creation of an interpretive centre. An agreement to settle the Africville residents' lawsuit was reached in February 2010. On February 24, 2010, more than forty years after the demolition of the area, an official apology was made on behalf of HRM. No action was taken on the matter of individual compensation. Most were optimistic and hopeful that a new era of respect and reconciliation was about to occur. Brenda Steed-Ross, who was evicted at eighteen along with her parents and infant daughter commented, "I feel like we're moving forward, not backward."

Canada has a mixed history of apologies to other oppressed groups. Some, such as Japanese-Canadians, interned during the Second World War, and First Nations who attended residential schools, were individually compensated for their suffering. But interned Italian-Canadians from the Second World War and descendants of passengers on the *Komagata Maru* were not compensated following their apology.

WATCH THE VIDEO

We're Sorry

Forty years after the relocation, Mayor Peter Kelly is shown here apologizing. "We realize words cannot undo what has been done. But we are profoundly sorry and apologize to each and every one of you. The repercussions of what happened to Africville linger to this day. They haunt us in the form of lost opportunities for the young people who never were nurtured in the rich traditions, culture and heritage of Africville . . . Our history cannot be rewritten but, thankfully, the future is a blank page and, starting today, we hold the pen with which we can write a shared tomorrow."

Watch the video at http://tinyurl.com/rcwafricville30

Was it Enough?
Along with the apology, Mayor Kelly promised $3 million towards the reconstruction of Seaview Church (a memorial to Africville), 2.5 acres at Seaview Park for the Africville Heritage Trust Board (land that is still owned by the city), a park maintenance agreement to be established between the Africville Heritage Trust and HRM for Seaview Park and the establishment of an African Nova Scotian Affairs Office within HRM.

An Apology for Africville

" On behalf of the Halifax Regional Municipality, I apologize to the former Africville residents and their descendants for what they have endured for almost 50 years, ever since the loss of their community that had stood on the shores of Bedford Basin for more than 150 years.

You lost your houses, your church, all of the places where you gathered with family and friends to mark the milestones of your lives.

For all that, we apologize.

We apologize to the community elders, including those who did not live to see this day, for the pain and loss of dignity you experienced.

We apologize to the generations who followed, for the deep wounds you have inherited and the way your lives were disrupted by the disappearance of your community.

We apologize for the heartache experienced at the loss of the Seaview United Baptist Church, the spiritual heart of the community, removed in the middle of the night. We acknowledge the tremendous importance the church had, both for the congregation and the community as a whole.

We realize words cannot undo what has been done, but we are profoundly sorry and apologize to all the former residents and their descendants.

The repercussions of what happened in Africville linger to this day. They haunt us in the form of lost opportunities for young people who were never nurtured in the rich traditions, culture and heritage of Africville.

They play out in lingering feelings of hurt and distrust, emotions that this municipality continues to work hard with the African Nova Scotian community to overcome.

For all the distressing consequences, we apologize.

Our history cannot be rewritten but, thankfully, the future is a blank page and, starting today, we hold the pen with which we can write a shared tomorrow.

It is in that spirit of respect and reconciliation that we ask your forgiveness."

WATCH THE VIDEO

Coming Together
The apology was delivered at the YMCA in North End Halifax. Mayor Kelly is pictured here with dignitaries and former residents. Reverend Rhonda Britten, a leader within the Nova Scotia Black community, stated, "I know that there are some among us who are wounded, and some among us who bear those scars. But, in spite of all of that, the victory has been won. We must forgive and must push forward."

Watch the video at
http://tinyurl.com/rcwafricville16

Resolution
The apology and the response of former Africville residents is a demonstration of the mutual desire for reconciliation as suggested by the United Nations Report of 2004.

The Halifax Apology 73

Permanent Acknowledgements

WATCH THE VIDEO

Africville is a powerful symbol in the fight against racism and segregation and in the ongoing struggle of African Canadians to defend their rights and culture in Nova Scotia. In addition to the physical expression of land, buildings and exhibits, have come creative expression in the form of music, literature, and art. Many national and international documentaries, books, magazine articles, TV and radio programs, poetry, plays and songs have made known the story of the destruction of Africville. The artists include singer-songwriters Faith Nolan, Joe Sealy and Trevor Mackenzie. Authors including George Boyd, George Elliott Clarke, Dorothy Perkyns, Donald Clairmont, Dennis Magill, Jon Tattrie and Stephens Gerard Malone have written about Africville.

Watch the video at
http://tinyurl.com/rcwafricville18

WATCH THE VIDEO

In Memory Of
In 1988, a monument was erected on the former Africville grounds to commemorate the first three Black settlers of Africville.

Watch the video at
http://tinyurl.com/rcwafricville36

WATCH THE VIDEO

CANADA

WATCH THE VIDEO

©2014

AFRICVILLE

63

Birchtown

The Birchtown Black Loyalist Heritage Centre opened in 2015 in Birchtown, NS. The interpretive centre tells the story of early Black Loyalist settlers who came to Nova Scotia, mainly Birchtown. Some of their descendants lived in Africville.

Watch the video at http://tinyurl.com/rcwafricville19

Commemorative Gesture

In January 2014, Canada Post released this stamp to commemorate Halifax's oldest and largest Black neighbourhood, Africville. "I'm thrilled," said Bernice Arsenault, one of seven girls pictured on the stamp. The photo was snapped in 1958 outside a Bible study class.

Watch the video at http://tinyurl.com/rcwafricville20

Permanent Acknowledgements

"... it is important to remember the terrible things that happened ..."

Important Replica

As part of the apology, this replica of the original Seaview United Baptist Church was completed in 2012 and dedicated as a museum and interpretive centre. Lindell Smith is Halifax City Councillor for District 8, which includes the former community of Africville. "The only reason that Africville is not here today is because of what the city did to the community. I think it's important to remember the terrible things that happened, the discrimination and displacement. But also the people of Africville had ownership and a sense of community, and that is something to celebrate."

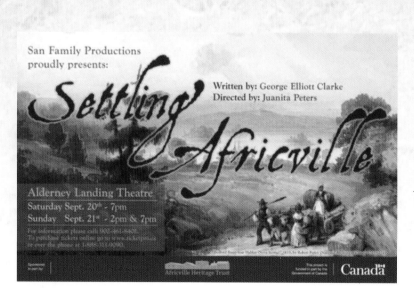

San Family Productions proudly presents:

Written by: George Elliott Clarke
Directed by: Juanita Peters

Settling Africville

Alderney Landing Theatre
Saturday Sept. 20th - 7pm
Sunday Sept. 21st - 2pm & 7pm

Canada

Tribute

In 2014 the Africville Heritage Trust commissioned author and playwright George Elliott Clarke to write the play *Settling Africville*. It was produced by San Family Productions and directed by Juanita Peters.

Important Marker

This monument marks the area of Tibby's Pond, which was on Tibby Alcock's property. This was where the children swam, rafted and in the winter, played hockey. It was also where Africville's non-commercial fishing boats were tied up.

WATCH THE VIDEO

Telling the Story

These exhibits inside the Africville Museum help recall the way of life of a thriving community that suffered over a hundred years of racism with dignity and faith.

Watch the video at
http://tinyurl.com/rcwafricville21

WATCH THE VIDEO

Joe Sealy

Africville Suite

Soulful Tribute

The album cover for *Africville Suite* by Joe Sealy is pictured here. His music won a Juno Award and he is a member of the Order of Canada.

Watch the video at http://tinyurl.com/rcwafricville37

C.N.R.

Africville Suite is in memory of his father, who was born in Africville.

Once a Home

In 1996, Montreal-born jazz pianist Joe Sealy created twelve musical pieces reflecting on places and activities in Africville, where his father was born. Joe Sealy lived in Halifax when Africville was destroyed.

Joe Sealy:

"When I found out about what they did and ... how they did it, the sneaky way that they conned people into getting off their properties, and the injustice of it all ... When I did my research, that's when I really got into the story and the story that really needed to be told."

WATCH THE VIDEO

Retain Your Culture

The story of Africville has influenced the work of Dr. George Elliott Clarke, a Nova Scotian poet, playwright and educator. He is quoted in this video attending the opening of the replica Seaview African United Baptist Church in 2011.

Watch the video at
http://tinyurl.com/rcwafricville23

George Elliott Clarke:
"Well, this is the beginning of a recovery of culture and history that had been neglected, which some thought that they could basically bulldoze away. I think it's a lesson to everyone that if you do not try to maintain your culture — if it's important — then it's very likely that you may lose it or others will try to take it away from you."

Permanent Acknowledgements

Controversy and Conflict

Controversy over the contentious 1960s-era decision to raze Africville continues. In November 2016, lawyer Robert Pineo contended that Halifax did not follow its own rules under the city's charter. When Mayor Kelly issued the apology in 2010, there were dissenting voices shouting, "Not enough." Some former residents and descendants claimed the settlement was illegal because the Africville Genealogy Society did not have authorization to negotiate on their behalf. Nowhere in the apology was there a mention of the role the city played in the destruction of the community. Anger was expressed over the provision for a replica church / interpretive centre, instead of a church where former residents and their descendants could hold weekly services or significant celebrations. The City of Halifax had avoided the larger issue of reparation — individual compensation. A group of former residents launched new court proceedings against Halifax City government. In 2015, Judge Patrick Duncan dismissed the claims of dozens of people, saying they signed on to the settlement agreement after getting legal advice and knowing the effect of the agreement. The Society had signed releases on behalf of forty-eight estates promising not to take the city to court again. As of 2018, forty-two people and nine estates were seeking individual compensation from the city. They are seeking fair market value for their properties. Tony Smith says, "I'm very excited to see that this is a very strong possibility after all these years, justice will finally get done and people will be vindicated."

Preserving the Past

Outside what looks like a regular church is, on the inside, a small museum with exhibits portraying what life was like in Africville from the 1800s to its demolition in the 1960s. Many former residents wanted their church replaced as part of the deal with the city. Instead a replica shell was built, with a museum, not a church, inside.

Staying Put

Eddie Carvery's trailer remained on the Africville site as a symbol of protest. Though offers came to him to purchase it as a cultural artifact, he held steadfast to keeping it on the site as a reminder that the fight is ongoing.

Watch the video at
http://tinyurl.com/rcwafricville24

WATCH THE VIDE

WATCH THE VIDEO

Marking the Spot

A young woman holds a sign denoting the former estate of James Hamilton where John Tolliver, two-time winner of the Golden Glove Boxing Award, lived. Ada Adams, who left Africville at the age of two, comes back every year with her children to show them her birthplace. "We should remember that this was a wonderful community. It was home to people."

▶ Watch the video at
http://tinyurl.com/rcwafricville26

"We should remember that this was a wonderful community. It was home to people."

WATCH THE VIDEO

SUPREME COURT OF NOVA SCOTIA
Citation: *Williams v. Halifax Regional Municipality,*
2015 NSSC 228

Date: 2015-07-30
Docket: *Hfx*, No. 126561
Registry: Halifax

Between:
Rosella Williams, Mildred Denise Allen, Donald Brown, Shirley Brown, April Carvery, Blenn Edward Carvery, David Bruce Carvery, Dean Carvery, Edward Carvery, Edward Bayfield Carvery, John Edward Carvery, Nelson Carvery, Rose Charlene Carvery, Victor W. Carvery, Yvonne Carvery, Marleen Bernice Cassidy, Donna Darlene Dixon, Leonard James Dixon, Debra Lee Emerson-DeLeon, Bernice Flint, Idella Marie Flint, Olive Flint, Raymond Patterson Flint, Sheila Flint, Warren Grant, Ronald W. Howe, Marie Louise Izzard-Carvery, Marjorie Carrie-Ann Izzard, Martina Izzard, Phillip Daniel Izzard, Shawn Izzard, Alfreda Peters, Roger Leslie Thomas, Craig Vemb, Fleming Vemb, Jean Vemb, Leo Vemb, Isabel Wareham, Teresa Patricia Williams (Carvery), Clarence Brown (deceased), Wennison Byers (deceased), Vera Carter (deceased), Bernadine Carvery (deceased), Rosalyn Carvery (deceased), Doramae Clayton (deceased), Wayne S. Dixon (deceased), Ernest Flint (deceased), Dr. Ruth B. Johnson (deceased), Jack Carvery (deceased), Morton Flint (deceased), Gerald J. Johnson (deceased), Irene Izzard (deceased), and Albert Kenneth Sparks (deceased)

Applicant

v.

The City of Halifax, a body corporate

Respondent

Judge: The Honourable Justice Patrick J. Duncan
Heard: February 25, 2015, in Halifax, Nova Scotia
Final Written Submissions: July 27, 2015
Counsel: Robert Pineo, Jeremy Smith and Michael Scott for the Applicants
Karen MacDonald and Martin Ward Q.C., for the Respondent

Still Protesting

Eddie Carvery poses with a copy of a book about him, titled *The Hermit of Africville*. "I'm here because I was born here. What they did to our community and to our ancestors, right up to today was illegal. It was immoral, it was wrong . . . There will be a protest until the Africville people have been dealt with fairly," he said in May 2018.

▶ Watch the videos at
http://tinyurl.com/rcwafricville27
http://tinyurl.com/rcwafricville28

An On-going Struggle

Splitting from the group of original plaintiffs after settlement was achieved, there is an on-going legal battle with the Halifax City government. Nelson Carvery, named in the above legal document, is the main plaintiff. "Well, it will bring closure when it's completed. We weren't properly compensated for our lands." Their initial application to launch a class action suit was denied in 2018.

Future Generations

The Africville story is often regarded as a flagrant example of racist attitudes and behaviour — a complete refusal to acknowledge what residents needed and still want. The Africville Genealogy Society is now demanding not only compensation, but restoration. The people want to go home again, to rebuild their community on the shores of the Bedford Basin. So the struggle continues. At the same time, rapid development of Halifax's downtown core and outlying areas continues, and even the well-established community of Uniacke Square is threatened by redevelopment. In other Black communities in HRM, such as Beechville, new development has replaced much of the original Black settlement. Without a conscious effort to preserve their character as Black areas, places such as Jelly Bean Square, East and North Preston, Lake Loon and Cherry Brook could disappear. Many residents in Nova Scotia's Black settlements are descendants of the Black Loyalists, and refugees of the War of 1812. They continue to battle the government for clear title and ownership of the land originally granted them by the government. It's estimated that a third of would-be property owners in the North Preston community still do not have legal documentation for land given to them in 1775 and 1812.

Moving Ahead
Olufemi Matthew Odusanya, an Africville descendant, is pictured here at his graduation from Nova Scotia Community College, Truro, NS. Unlike Olufemi, some Black youth do not have the funds to further their education. That is why the Africville Heritage Trust set up a scholarship fund for former residents and their descendants. The law firm Waterbury Newton donated $100,000 from a portion of legal fees they received in the settling of an action against the former City of Halifax.

New Generations
Irvine Carvery's grandchildren, Mila Rose and Karter, provide him with continued motivation to work for a better legacy for former Africville residents.

Many Celebrations
Former Africville residents and descendants continue to organize events, such as this inter-generational event in 2017, to keep the memories alive for the next generation and to show continued support for each other.

Not Affordable For All
In North End Halifax, still an economically deprived area, rent is creeping higher, making new apartments unattainable for most families.

New development has replaced much of the original Black settlement.

Change Everywhere
New developments are taking over Gottingen Street, Halifax, once the heart of the urban Black community where many Africville residents relocated. These projects create new pressures on low-income residents who are at risk of being forced out of the area.

Listen to the audio at
http://tinyurl.com/rcwafricville29

LISTEN TO THE AUDIO

The Push
Gentrification of the area is reflected in advertising aimed at investors and higher-income people in the redevelopment of Halifax's Gottingen Street.

Being Supplanted
Expensive lofts and condos are making the downtown area an attractive place to live. Current residents ponder and protest against what the future holds for them.

Out With the Old
When the transformation of Halifax's Gottingen Street is completed, property values and rents will be much higher. Low-income families and small businesses will be displaced — again.

Racism Continues

Nova Scotia Senator Wanda Thomas Bernard, pictured here, says, "A recent report on anti-Black racism in Canada from the United Nations Working Group of Experts on People of African Descent validates the experience of African Nova Scotians ... the inequities between African Nova Scotian students and other Nova Scotian students remains unchanged decades after integration. The report called the socioeconomic conditions of Black communities in the province 'deplorable.' The historical context of slavery and segregation has created the current circumstances of systemic anti-Black racism." Referencing the United Nations report and based on her experiences of anti-Black racism as an African Nova Scotian woman, a social worker, a researcher, an educator and now a senator, she called for an inquiry into anti-Black racism in Canada in May 2018.

In June 2018, HRM released a progress report on discrimination and racism in the workplace. A number of public protests and human rights rulings had highlighted issues with city departments including Metro Transit, the fire service and the public works department.

Searching For Answers

In 2017, Keith Colwell, member of Nova Scotia's Legislative Assembly (MLA) for the Prestons, shown above, said, "There's nobody encroaching on the properties that I'm aware of in these areas. It's just strictly a matter of land titles." In September 2017, the Nova Scotia government announced that it would provide $2.7 million to help people in five historically Black communities — North Preston, East Preston, Cherry Brook, Lincolnville and Sunnyville — gain formal legal ownership of land they've actually owned for generations.

A Matter of Time

This community sign proclaims North Preston as the "Largest Black Community in Canada." Irvine Carvery says the lack of legal ownership documents is impacting the future development of the community. Dwight Adams of the North Preston Land Recovery Initiative complains that the province is not investing enough. "Each community should be asking for more ... It's not just this community that needs it. It's not just the five that stepped up that are in the forefront of the conversation. It's all the communities."

Timeline

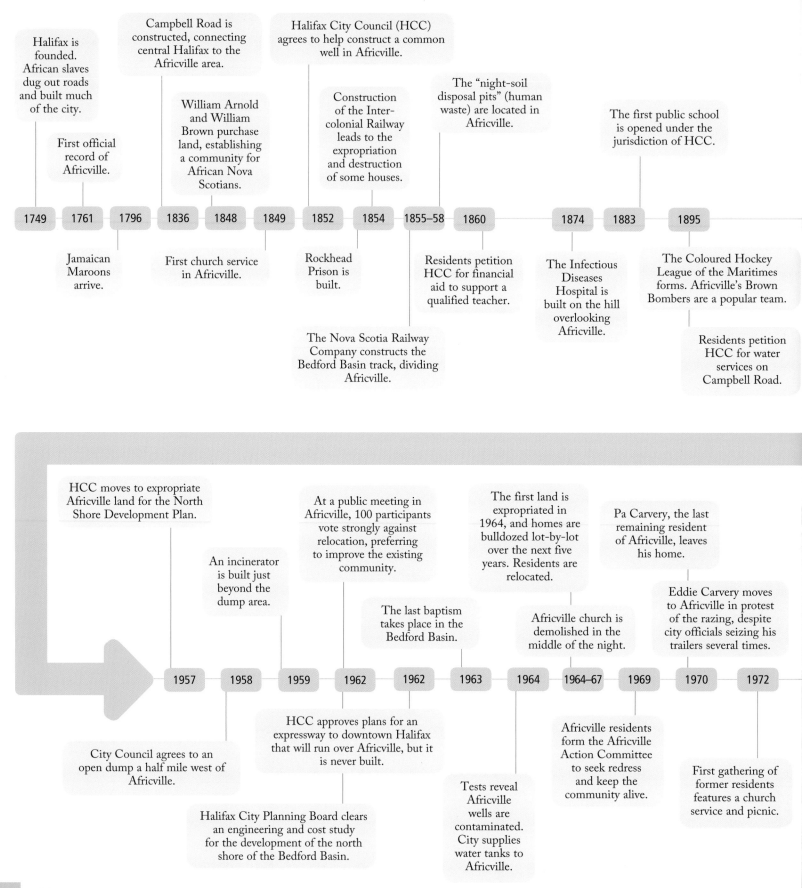

1749 — Halifax is founded. African slaves dug out roads and built much of the city.

1761 — First official record of Africville.

Jamaican Maroons arrive.

1796 — Campbell Road is constructed, connecting central Halifax to the Africville area.

1836 — William Arnold and William Brown purchase land, establishing a community for African Nova Scotians.

First church service in Africville.

1848

1849 — Halifax City Council (HCC) agrees to help construct a common well in Africville.

1852 — Construction of the Inter-colonial Railway leads to the expropriation and destruction of some houses.

Rockhead Prison is built.

1854 — The Nova Scotia Railway Company constructs the Bedford Basin track, dividing Africville.

1855–58 — The "night-soil disposal pits" (human waste) are located in Africville.

1860 — Residents petition HCC for financial aid to support a qualified teacher.

1874 — The Infectious Diseases Hospital is built on the hill overlooking Africville.

1883 — The first public school is opened under the jurisdiction of HCC.

1895 — The Coloured Hockey League of the Maritimes forms. Africville's Brown Bombers are a popular team.

Residents petition HCC for water services on Campbell Road.

1957 — HCC moves to expropriate Africville land for the North Shore Development Plan.

1958 — City Council agrees to an open dump a half mile west of Africville.

1959 — An incinerator is built just beyond the dump area.

1962 — At a public meeting in Africville, 100 participants vote strongly against relocation, preferring to improve the existing community.

HCC approves plans for an expressway to downtown Halifax that will run over Africville, but it is never built.

1962 — The last baptism takes place in the Bedford Basin.

Halifax City Planning Board clears an engineering and cost study for the development of the north shore of the Bedford Basin.

1963 — The first land is expropriated in 1964, and homes are bulldozed lot-by-lot over the next five years. Residents are relocated.

1964 — Tests reveal Africville wells are contaminated. City supplies water tanks to Africville.

1964–67 — Africville church is demolished in the middle of the night.

1969 — Pa Carvery, the last remaining resident of Africville, leaves his home.

Africville residents form the Africville Action Committee to seek redress and keep the community alive.

1970 — Eddie Carvery moves to Africville in protest of the razing, despite city officials seizing his trailers several times.

1972 — First gathering of former residents features a church service and picnic.

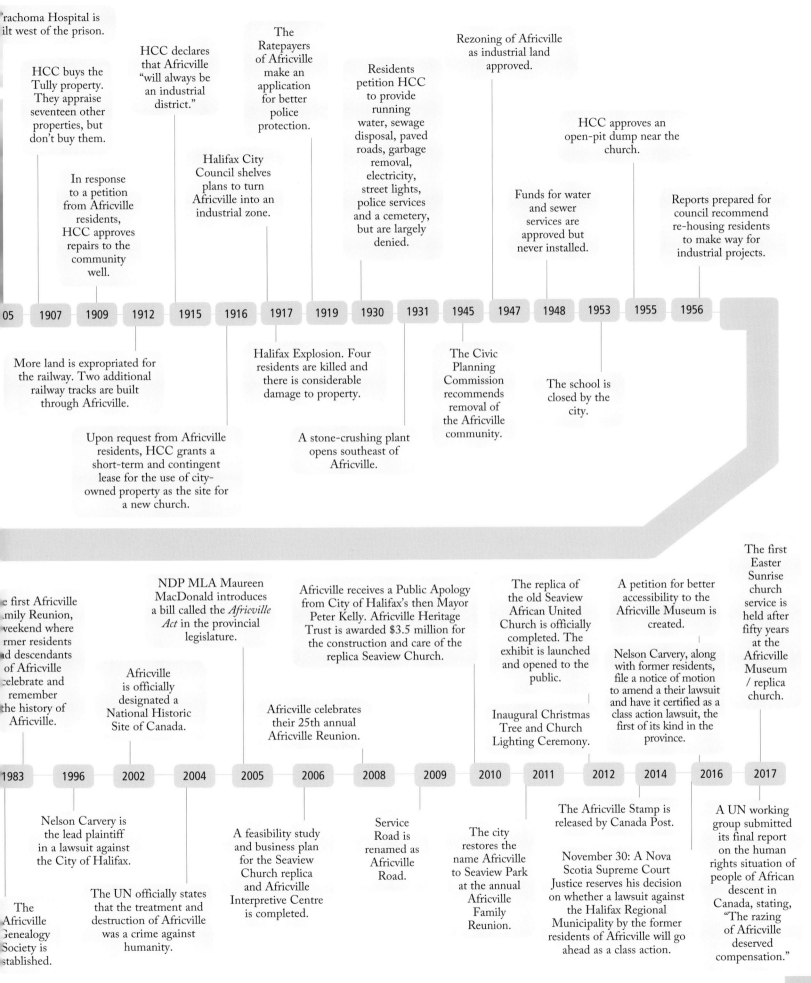

Trachoma Hospital is built west of the prison.

HCC buys the Tully property. They appraise seventeen other properties, but don't buy them.

In response to a petition from Africville residents, HCC approves repairs to the community well.

HCC declares that Africville "will always be an industrial district."

Halifax City Council shelves plans to turn Africville into an industrial zone.

The Ratepayers of Africville make an application for better police protection.

Residents petition HCC to provide running water, sewage disposal, paved roads, garbage removal, electricity, street lights, police services and a cemetery, but are largely denied.

Rezoning of Africville as industrial land approved.

HCC approves an open-pit dump near the church.

Funds for water and sewer services are approved but never installed.

Reports prepared for council recommend re-housing residents to make way for industrial projects.

05 | 1907 | 1909 | 1912 | 1915 | 1916 | 1917 | 1919 | 1930 | 1931 | 1945 | 1947 | 1948 | 1953 | 1955 | 1956

More land is expropriated for the railway. Two additional railway tracks are built through Africville.

Upon request from Africville residents, HCC grants a short-term and contingent lease for the use of city-owned property as the site for a new church.

Halifax Explosion. Four residents are killed and there is considerable damage to property.

A stone-crushing plant opens southeast of Africville.

The Civic Planning Commission recommends removal of the Africville community.

The school is closed by the city.

The first Africville Family Reunion, a weekend where former residents and descendants of Africville celebrate and remember the history of Africville.

NDP MLA Maureen MacDonald introduces a bill called the *Africville Act* in the provincial legislature.

Africville is officially designated a National Historic Site of Canada.

Africville receives a Public Apology from City of Halifax's then Mayor Peter Kelly. Africville Heritage Trust is awarded $3.5 million for the construction and care of the replica Seaview Church.

Africville celebrates their 25th annual Africville Reunion.

The replica of the old Seaview African United Church is officially completed. The exhibit is launched and opened to the public.

Inaugural Christmas Tree and Church Lighting Ceremony.

A petition for better accessibility to the Africville Museum is created.

Nelson Carvery, along with former residents, file a notice of motion to amend a their lawsuit and have it certified as a class action lawsuit, the first of its kind in the province.

The first Easter Sunrise church service is held after fifty years at the Africville Museum / replica church.

1983 | 1996 | 2002 | 2004 | 2005 | 2006 | 2008 | 2009 | 2010 | 2011 | 2012 | 2014 | 2016 | 2017

The Africville Genealogy Society is established.

Nelson Carvery is the lead plaintiff in a lawsuit against the City of Halifax.

The UN officially states that the treatment and destruction of Africville was a crime against humanity.

A feasibility study and business plan for the Seaview Church replica and Africville Interpretive Centre is completed.

Service Road is renamed as Africville Road.

The city restores the name Africville to Seaview Park at the annual Africville Family Reunion.

The Africville Stamp is released by Canada Post.

November 30: A Nova Scotia Supreme Court Justice reserves his decision on whether a lawsuit against the Halifax Regional Municipality by the former residents of Africville will go ahead as a class action.

A UN working group submitted its final report on the human rights situation of people of African descent in Canada, stating, "The razing of Africville deserved compensation."

Glossary

Abattoir: A place where animals are killed in order to provide meat.

Acadian: Descendants of French colonists who settled in Acadia during the seventeenth and eighteenth centuries.

Activism: Vigorous action or involvement as a means of achieving political or other goals, sometimes by demonstrations, protests, etc.

Advocate: A person who publicly supports or recommends a particular cause or policy and who may put a case forward on someone else's behalf.

African Diaspora: Peoples of African origin living outside the continent, regardless of their citizenship and nationality.

African Nova Scotians: Black Canadians whose ancestors primarily date back to the Colonial United States as slaves or free persons, and later arrived in Nova Scotia during the eighteenth and early nineteenth centuries.

Amenities: Something that helps to provide comfort, convenience or enjoyment.

Auxiliary class: A separate class or lesson in school to give extra help and support.

Bias: A preference or tendency to think or act in a certain way. Could be positive or negative.

Civil Rights: The basic privileges that come with being a member of society in a certain country. This may include a right to vote, to have an education, to receive justice in the courts.

Compensation: The payment of money to make up for a wrong that was done to a person or group.

Culture: The way of life of a group of people and how they interact with their surroundings. Culture is considered a distinguishing feature of a group, but individuals within a group can be diverse.

Deed: A legal document that is signed and delivered, especially one regarding the ownership of property or legal rights.

Deportation: The sending away of people from the country where they are living back to the country from whence they came.

Desegregation: Ending the separation of different racial, religious or cultural groups.

Diaspora: The movement or spread of people away from their homeland.

Discrimination: Unjust actions that are caused by a particular mindset or prejudice, a means of treating people negatively because of their group identity. Discrimination may be based on age, ancestry, gender, language, race, religion, political beliefs, sexual orientation, family status, physical or mental disability, appearance or economic status.

Displaced: To force something or someone out of its usual or original position.

Domestic: A servant who is paid to perform menial tasks around the household.

Emigration: Leaving one's home country to go to a different country.

Environmental racism: A type of discrimination where people of low-income or minority communities are forced to live in close proximity to environmentally hazardous or degraded environments, such as toxic waste, pollution and urban decay.

Exhibit: To show an object or collection of objects publicly, especially for purposes of competition, education or demonstration.

Expropriation: Seizure of land, property, etc., from its owner with little or no compensation.

First Nations: Aboriginal Canadians who are not ethnically Métis or Inuit. This term came into common usage in the 1970s and 1980s and generally replaced the term "Indian," although unlike "Indian," the term "First Nation" does not have a legal definition. Singular "First Nation" can refer to a band, a reserve-based community or a larger tribal grouping and the Status Indians who live in them.

Genealogy: The study of the history of the past and present members of a family or families.

Gentrification: The process of wealthier residents moving to an area that is already populated with lower-income residents and the changes that occur due to the influx of wealth.

Heritage: Traditions passed down to younger generations.

Immigration: The arrival of people into a country from their homeland.

Injustice: A wrongful action taken against an individual or group that denies them their basic rights.

Integration: Combining one group into another, such as a racial, ethnic or religious group.

Land Grant: A government transfer of public property to an individual or group.

Loyalists: A person who is a loyal supporter of the sovereign or of the existing government, especially in time of revolt. The Black Loyalists who came to Nova Scotia supported the British rule.

Marginalized: Placed in a position of lesser importance, influence or power.

Migration: To move from one country, place, or locality to another.

Mi'kmaq: A member of the Algonquian people (First Nations People) inhabiting the Maritime Provinces of Canada.

Negotiate: Have formal discussions in order to reach an agreement.

Oppression: When the feelings, ideas or demands of an individual or group of people are not recognized or allowed to be expressed by authorities, such as the government, justice system, police or military.

Petition: A formal request bearing the names of those making the request to people in authority soliciting some favour, right, mercy or other benefit.

Plaintiff: A person who brings a legal action in a court.

Plantation: A large farm or estate on which cotton, tobacco, coffee, sugar cane or the like is cultivated, in many cases, by unpaid labourers.

Prejudice: An attitude, usually negative, directed towards a person or group of people based on wrong or distorted information. Prejudiced thinking may result in acts of discrimination.

Protest: A statement or action expressing disapproval of, or objection to, something.

Racism: A belief that one race is superior to another. People are not treated as equals because of their culture or ethnic differences. Racism may be systemic (part of institutions, governments, organizations and programs) or part of the attitudes and behaviours of individuals.

Raze: To tear down, demolish or level to the ground.

Reconciliation: An act to restore to friendship or harmony, as when former enemies agree to an amicable truce.

Redress: To right a wrong, sometimes by compensating the victims or by punishing the wrong-doer. Refers to the movement within the Africville community for an official apology and payment for the injustices of the government's actions towards the Africville community in the 1960s.

Refugees: People who leave a country for fear of persecution based on race, religion, political opinion or nationality.

Relocation: The action of moving to a new place and establishing one's home or business there.

Second-class: Of the class, rank, excellence, etc., next below the highest; of secondary quality.

Segregation: The policy or practice of separating people of different races, classes or ethnic groups, especially as a form of discrimination.

Slavery: The ownership, buying and selling of humans, mostly Black Africans, as objects or property, mainly for labour.

Slum: A thickly populated area in a city marked by crowding, run-down housing, poverty and social disorganization.

Social assistance: Money provided by the government to help people who are in poverty.

Trustee: Any person or board appointed to manage the affairs of an institution or organization such as a church.

Urban renewal: A term popularly used in the 1940s–1970s for measures to purchase, often by expropriation, and demolish areas where buildings (homes or other buildings) were considered in poor condition and replace them with new construction, including high-rise apartments, shopping centres and other building types. Urban renewal plans were developed and implemented by municipal governments, and paid for by cities, provinces and the federal government. Urban renewal funded by Ottawa halted because of strong resistance from area residents in Canadian cities and evidence that it was better housing and social policy to repair and improve both private buildings and city services rather than undertake wholesale area demolition. Redevelopment of urban areas continues to the present, but is not usually termed urban renewal.

Values: Beliefs that are considered important by an individual or a culture.

For Further Reading

Books:

Boyd, George. *Consecrated Ground*. Vancouver: Talon Books, 2011.

Clairmont, Donald H. and Dennis William Magill. *Africville Relocation Report*. Halifax: Halifax Institute of Public Affairs, Dalhousie University, 1971.

Clairmont, Donald H. and Dennis William Magill. *Africville: The Life and Death of a Canadian Black Community*. Toronto: Canadian Scholar's Press, 1999.

Delmore "Buddy" Daye Learning Institute. *The Times of African Nova Scotians, A Celebration of Our History, Heritage and Culture, Revised Edition*. Halifax: Delmore "Buddy" Daye Learning Institute, Volume One, 2014, Volume Two, 2015.

Flemming, David B. *Explosion in Halifax Harbour: The Illustrated Account of a Disaster that Shook the World*. Halifax: Formac Publishing, 2004.

Grant, John. *Black Nova Scotians*. Halifax: Nimbus Publishing, 1994.

Malone, Stephens Gerard. *Big Town*. Halifax: Vagrant Press / Nimbus, 2011.

Nelson, Jennifer. *Razing Africville: A Geography of Racism*. Toronto: University of Toronto Press, 2009.

Pachai, Bridglal. *Beneath the Clouds of the Promised Land, The Survival of Nova Scotia's Blacks, Volume 1, 1600-1800*. Halifax: Black Educators Association, 1987.

Pachai, Bridglal. *Beneath the Clouds of the Promised Land, The Survival of Nova Scotia's Blacks, Volume 2, 1800-1989*. Halifax: Black Educators Association, 1990.

Perkyns, Dorothy. *Last Days in Africville*. Toronto: Dundurn Press, 2006.

Reed, Blair. *1917 Halifax Explosion And American Response*. Halifax: Nimbus Publishing, 1999.

Robertson, Marion. *King's Bounty, A History of Early Shelburne, Nova Scotia*. Halifax: Nova Scotia Museum, 1983.

Tattrie, Jon. *The Hermit of Africville, The Life of Eddie Carvery*. Lawrencetown Beach: Pottersfield Press, 2010.

Taylor, Wanda. *Birchtown and the Black Loyalists*. Halifax: Nimbus Publishing, 2015.

The Africville Genealogy Society. *The Spirit of Africville, Second Edition*. Halifax: Formac Publishing, 2010.

Tolliver, Althea J. and James A. Francois. *From Africville to New Road: How Four Communities Planned their Development*. Halifax: McCurdy Printing & Typesetting Ltd., 1983.

Vincer, Mary Pamela. *A History of Marginalization — Africville: A Canadian Example of Forced Migration*. Toronto: Ryerson University, 2008.

Welldon, Christine. *Children of Africville*. Halifax: Nimbus Publishing, 2013.

Whitehead, Ruth Holmes. *Black Loyalists, Southern Settlers of Nova Scotia's First Free Black Communities*. Halifax: Nimbus Publishing, 2013.

Online Videos:

"Africville: Then and Now," March 9, 2015: www.youtube.com/watch?v=TBbrSCw8dCs

CBC, "Africville is Destroyed," September 15, 1967: www.cbc.ca/archives/entry/africville-is-destroyed

Lourme, Sophia, "Destruction Of Africville," March 29, 2016: www.youtube.com/watch?v=dYTAuTAxYZY

McGuinn, Charlotte. "The Story of Africville," November 27, 2016: www.youtube.com/watch?v=4763qJjALlw

"Racism in Halifax, 1962," July 28, 2010: www.youtube.com/watch?v=qZ2OM03mtmg

Tattrie, Jon, "Eddie Carvery in Africville, Nova Scotia," December 20, 2010: www.youtube.com/watch?v=Q8ofNn8e_ik

Plays, Movies and Videos:

Africville: Can't Stop Now, a documentary produced by Marty Williams and directed by Juanita Peters, 2010.

Remember Africville, a video directed by Shelagh Mackenzie. Halifax: National Film Board. Atlantic Centre, 1991.

Settling Africville, a play by playwright and poet George Elliott Clarke, directed by Juanita Peters, 2014.

Visual Credits

Every effort has been made to locate the original copyright owners. If the reader has any additional information on the original copyright owners, we would be happy to include it in any revised editions.

Africville Museum: p. 69 (right)

Air'leth Aodhfin, reprinted from *The WholeNote* by permission of the photographer: p. 9 (bottom)

Ardith Pye: p. 35 (cover & middle)

Artist Dr. Ruth Johnson, 1949: p. 69 (left)

Beneath the Clouds of the Promised Land, The Survival of Nova Scotia's Blacks, Volume 2, 1800-1989 by Bridglal Pachai; Black Educators Association, 1990: p. 41 (top left), p. 42 (top & bottom left), p. 63 (bottom)

Birchtown and the Black Loyalists by Wanda Taylor; Nimbus Publishing, 2015: p. 12

Black Cultural Centre for Nova Scotia: p. 39 (top).

Black Nova Scotians by John Grant; Nimbus Publishing, 1994: p. 19 (bottom), p. 40 (left)

© Canada Post Corporation, 2014. Reproduced with permission: p. 75 (bottom)

City of Halifax: p. 72 (left), p. 73

City of Toronto Archives: p. 22 (top, Fonds 1244, Item 2451)

Clara Adams: p. 41 (top right)

Delvina Bernard/Dan O'Brien: p. 68-69

Diene, Doubou. "Racism, Racial Discrimmination, Xenophobia and All Forms of Discrimmination." Report for the United Nations Economic and Social Council: 1 March 2004: p. 70 (right)

Donna James: p. 35 (top), p. 49 (top right), p. 50 (inset), p. 68 (bottom right)

Dr. Henry Bishop: p. 65 (bottom left)

Earl Conrad Collection: p. 41 (bottom left)

Evelyn Lawrence Collection: p. 41 (cover & bottom right)

Gloria Wesley Collection: p. 14 (bottom right), p. 61 (top, bottom left), p. 62 (bottom), p. 63 (top), p. 65 (top right, inset, bottom right) p. 70 (left), p. 75 (top), p. 76, p. 77, p. 80, p. 81 (top, bottom right), p. 82 (bottom right), p. 83, p. 84, p. 85 (bottom)

Habitat, March-April 1959: p. 48 (left)

Halifax Municipal Archives: p. 46 (right, 102-1B-1909-09), p. 48 (right, 711.45.S8)
    Atlantic Air Survey, 1962-03-21: p. 49 (top left, 102-39-1-411)

Halifax Police Department photograph: p. 59 (102-16N-0039.1)
    Reference Collection: p. 45 (bottom, 711.45.H17), p. 48 (right, 711.45.S8)

Irvine Carvery: p. 82 (bottom left)

Jesse Cain Collection: p. 37 (inset)

Kathleen Odusanya: p. 82 (top)

Keith Vaughan: p. 65 (cover & top left), p. 66 (cover, top right & inset)

Library and Archives Canada: p. 15 (top, Acc. No. 1938-220-1), p. 30 (top, PA-170741)
    C.M.H.C./Library and Archives Canada: p. 4 (PA-170736), p. 57 (top, PA-170739)
    Ted Grant/Library and Archives Canada: p. 7 (cover & bottom, PA-170247), p. 8 (top), p. 9 (top), p. 21 (top & middle), p. 26 (bottom right), p. 28 (inset), p. 29, p. 30 (cover & bottom, PA-), p. 31, p. 33 (bottom, PA-170253), p. 34 (main, PA-), p. 36 (top, PA-211060), p. 37 (top), p. 38 (top), p. 42 (bottom right), p. 43-44, p. 50 (right), p. 52 (top), p. 53 (left), p. 54, p. 54-55 (e002283009), p. 55, p. 56 (top), p. 64 (bottom)
    W.H. Coverdale Collection of Canadiana: p. 13 (top right, Acc. No. 1970-188-1090)

Mr. Robert Pineo: p. 51 (bottom left)

National Film Board of Canada, *Canada's Visual History*: p. 28 (main image)

Nelson Carvery: p. 58

Nick Pearce, Dalhousie University: p. 79

Nova Scotia Archives: p. 8 (bottom), p. 17 (middle, 1979-147, no. 468), p. 18, p. 19 (top), p. 22 (bottom, N-1268), p. 23 (top, 1989-298 / N-7081), p. 50 (left), p. 71 (top, 201800054)
    Acadian Recorder: p. 14 (left, 3 September 1814 p.3 microfilm no. 5193)
    Albert Lee Photography: p. 43 (bottom right)
    B. Edwards, *The Proceedings of the Governor and Assembly of Jamaica*: p. 13 (bottom, N-6202)
    Black Cultural Centre: 21 (bottom, George H. Craig)
    Bob Brooks Collection: p. 7 (cover & top, 1989-468 vol. 16 / sheet 4 image 17), p. 25 (top, 1989-468 vol. 16 / sheet 5 image 8), p. 25 (bottom), p. 26 (top right), p. 26 (left), p. 27 (right), p. 36 (bottom, 1989-468 vol. 16 / sheet 5 image 36), p. 39 (bottom left, 1989-468 vol. 16 / sheet 7 image 15), p. 43 (top), p. 47 (bottom, 1989-468 vol. 16 / sheet 4 image 33), p. 49 (bottom, 1989-468 vol. 16 / sheet 5 image 25), p. 51 (top), p. 51 (bottom right, 1989-468 vol. 16 /

sheet 11 image 27), p. 52 (bottom, 1989-468 vol. 16 / sheet 5 image 30), p. 53 (right, 1989-468 vol. 16 / sheet 7 image 25), p. 56-57 (1989-468 vol. 16 / sheet 4 image 34)
Documentary Art Collection: p. 13 (top left, 1979-147/56 | N-6955 CN-9813)
Halifax Gazette: p. 11 (top right, 30 May 1752 p. 2 microfilm no. 8152)
Helen Creighton: p. 47 (top, 1987-178 album 12 no. 26-27)
Joseph S. Rogers: p. 17 (bottom, *Rogers' Photographic Advertising Album* 1871 p. 18 / 1029/418)
Journal of the House of Assembly 1815: p. 15 (bottom, p. 107 microfilm no. 3528)
Kings County probate records estate: p. 17 (top, case file B7 microfilm no. 19779)
Nortman Studio: p. 34 (inset, 1983-310/2573), p. 44 (O/S no. 100053)
Robert Norwood: p. 32 (top left, 1987-480/263 | N-632)
Robert S. Low: p. 23 (bottom, 1992-524)
R.V. Harris: p. 45 (top, 1992-415 no. 5)
Nova Scotia Legislature: p. 85 (top right)
Office of Senator Wanda Thomas Bernard: p. 85 (top left)
Office of the Mayor of Halifax: p. 72 (right)
Ray and Evelyn Lawrence: p. 35 (bottom)
Ruth Johnson Collection, Earl Conrad: p. 32 (bottom)
Sergeant Craig Smith: p. 68 (top)
Slavery: Real people and their stories of enslavement edited by Reg Grant; Dorling Kindersley, London, 2009: p. 10, p. 11
Stanley and Ruth Carvery: p. 39 (bottom)
Stanley Carvery Collection: p. 67 (top)
Stephen Archibald: p. 24 (top)
Supreme Court of Nova Scotia: p. 81 (bottom left)
The Other Halifax Explosion: Bedford Magazine July 18-20, 1945 researched and compiled by H. Millard Wright in cooperation with CFAD Bedford: p. 22 (inset)
The Spirit of Africville by Africville Genealogy Society with contributions by Donald Clairmont, Stephen Kimber, Bridglal Pachai and Charles Saunders, Formac Publishing, Halifax, 2010: p. 14 (top right), p. 20, p. 24 (bottom), p. 32 (top right), p. 38 (bottom), p. 61 (bottom right), p. 62 (bottom right), p. 64 (bottom right), p. 67 (bottom), p. 71 (bottom), p. 74
The Times of African Nova Scotians, A Celebration of Our History, Heritage and Culture, Volume One, Delmore "Buddy" Daye Learning Institute, Halifax, 2014: p. 40 (right), p. 46 (left)
The Times of African Nova Scotians, A Celebration of Our History, Heritage and Culture, Volume Two, Delmore "Buddy" Daye Learning Institute, Halifax, 2015: p. 66 (bottom)
Tony Smith: p. 33 (top right)

Triplet Records: p. 78
Wartime Halifax by William D. Neftel: p. 33 (top left)
Wikipedia Creative Commons: p. 16, p. 60

Textual Credits

Quote by Eddie Carvery is from:
Tavlin, Noah. "Africville: Canada's Secret Racist History."
VICE News. February 4, 2013.

Quotes by Tony Smith are from:
Kennedy, Grace. "Africville: a community lost." *East Coast Post*.
February 4, 2016.

Quote by Stan Carvery is from:
Mellor, Clare. "Africville Museum aglow with lights for
Christmas and remembrance." *The Chronicle Herald*.
November 29, 2014.

Quote by Africville Relocatee is from:
Halifax Municipal Archives. City Clerk's Office records.
Historical reference files: Africville. Retrieval code:
102-5-1-44. 1965-1994.

Quote by Sergeant Craig Smith is from:
"The 20th Anniversary of the Halifax Race Riots." *The Apricity*.
July 13, 2011.

Quote by Joe Sealy is from:
Dagan, Ori. "Africville Revisited — Joe Sealy and Jackie
Richardson." *The WholeNote*. January 30, 2013.

Quote by George Elliott Clarke is from:
Brunhuber, Kim. "Remembering Africville." *CBC Video*.
September 25, 2011.

Quote by Mayor Walter Fitzgerald is from:
Vincer, Mary Pamela. "A History of Marginalization —
Africville: a Canadian Example of Forced Migration." *Ryerson
University*. Ryerson University Digital Commons Theses and
Dissertations.

The following people quoted are attributed to:
Africville Genealogy Society. *The Spirit of Africville*. Halifax:
Formac Publishing Company, 2010.
— Irvine Carvery
— Clarence Carvery
— Aaron Carvery
— Deborah Dixon-Jones
— Nova Scotia Education Minister Ron Giffin

Cox, Kevin. "Children fished and picked flowers years ago in hot
Africville summers." *The Globe and Mail*. July 6, 2002.
— Jaden Dixon
— Dr. Ruth Johnson (p. 61)
— Ada Adams

Pachai, Bridglal. *Beneath the Clouds of the Promised Land, The
Survival of Nova Scotia's Blacks, Volume 2, 1800-1989*. Halifax:
Black Educators Association, 1990.
— Dr. Ruth Johnson (p. 32 and 33)
— Elsie Desmond
— Leo Carvery

"The Story of Africville." *The Canadian Museum for Human
Rights*. February 23, 2017.
humanrights.ca/blog/black-history-month-story-africville
— Sunday Miller
— Lindell Smith

More books in the Righting Canada's Wrongs series

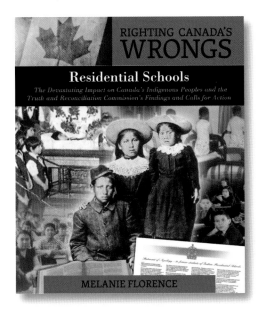

Residential Schools: The Devastating Impact on Canada's Indigenous Peoples and the Truth and Reconciliation Commission's Findings and Calls for Action

MELANIE FLORENCE

The story of Canada's residential school system for Indigenous young people and its impact on the students who attended and the communities they were from is explained in this highly visual book. This book features first-person accounts by survivors, excerpts from the Truth and Reconciliation Commission report, full text of the federal government's 2008 apology and key recommendations from the 94 Calls to Action by the Truth and Reconciliation Commission.

★ Ontario Library Association's Best Bets Young Adult Non-Fiction
★ CCBC Best Books for Kids and Teens — Starred Selection
★ One of the Year's Best — Resource Links

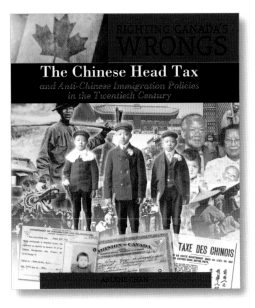

The Chinese Head Tax and Anti-Chinese Immigration Policies in the Twentieth Century

ARLENE CHAN

A detailed account of institutional racism, including a head tax and an immigration ban imposed in 1923 that lasted more than twenty years, to limit Chinese immigration to Canada. Despite lasting hostility and racism, Chinese-Canadians continued to build their communities and the federal government apologized for these racist policies in 2008.

★ Nominated for the Red Cedar Children's Choice Award
★ Nominated for the Heritage Toronto Book Award
★ CCBC Best Books for Kids and Teens — Starred Selection

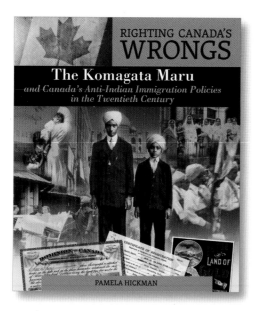

The Komagata Maru and Canada's Anti-Indian Immigration Policies in the Twentieth Century

PAMELA HICKMAN

A visual history of the courageous Indians who sailed to Vancouver to start a new life — only to be turned away by a racist immigration policy — and the experiences of other Indian citizens who were successful in their efforts to come to Canada.

Italian Canadian Internment in the Second World War

PAMELA HICKMAN AND JEAN SMITH CAVALLUZZO

A detailed history of the prejudice and racism that set the stage for a roundup and internment of hundreds of Italian Canadians during the Second World War, the lasting impact on future generations, and the community's successful demand for an apology from the federal government.

★ One of the Year's Best — Resource Links
★ CCBC Best Books for Kids and Teens — Starred Selection
★ Longlisted for the Information Book Award

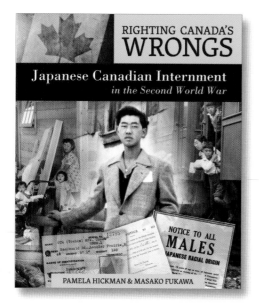

Japanese Canadian Internment in the Second World War

PAMELA HICKMAN AND MASAKO FUKAWA

A detailed account of the wartime hysteria that erupted after Japan attacked Pearl Harbour during the Second World War. More than 20,000 Japanese Canadians had their civil rights, homes, possessions, and freedom revoked despite being established in communities mainly in BC. After years of pressure, the federal government apologized for this historic wrong.

★ One of the Year's Best — Resource Links